SCHOLASTIC

Primary French in Practice

TERMS AND CONDITIONS

IMPORTANT – PERMITTED USE AND WARNINGS – READ CAREFULLY BEFORE USING

Minimum specification:

- PC or Mac with a CD-ROM drive and at least 512 Mb of RAM
- Recommended screen resolution: 1024 x768 pixels. (See CD-ROM help notes for details.)
- Facilities for printing

PC:

- Windows 2000 or XP or above
- Recommended minimum processor speed: 600 MHz
- 16 bit sound and 3D graphics card

Mac:

- Mac OSX.2 or above
- Recommended minimum processor speed: 500 MHz

For all technical support queries, please phone Scholastic Customer Services on 0845 603 9091.

OR AGES
5-11

collaboration with

Author
Paul Rogers

Development Editor
Kate Pedlar

Project Editor
Fabia Lewis

Illustrators
Origin 3D Ltd

Series Designers
Melissa Leeke
Helen Taylor

CD-ROM
developed in association
with Manic Monkey Ltd

Published by Scholastic Ltd
Villiers House
Clarendon Avenue
Leamington Spa
Warwickshire CV32 5PR

www.scholastic.co.uk

Designed using Adobe InDesign

Printed by Bell and Bain Ltd, Glasgow

1 2 3 4 5 6 7 8 9   8 9 0 1 2 3 4 5 6

Text © 2008, Paul Rogers

© 2008, Scholastic Ltd

British Library Cataloguing-in-Publication Data
A catalogue record for this book is available from the
British Library

ISBN 978-1407-10092-0

Contents

Resources on the CD-ROM 5

How to use the CD-ROM 6

Introduction 8

Why teach a foreign language? 8

Why French? 9

What do I have to teach? 10

Choosing resources and materials 11

Part 1 What do I need to know about language teaching? 12

How long and how often? 12

How do I provide enough practice? 13

How do I recycle material? 14

How can I improve pronunciation? 14

How can I develop communication? 16

How do I encourage children to ask and answer questions? 18

How important is learning by heart? 19

How should I use French in the classroom? 20

Is grammar important? 21

How should the teaching of grammar be approached? 22

The balance between encouragement and correction 26

At what point should reading and writing be introduced? 27

The four skills 28

Using stories 28

Using songs 30

What is 'communicative language teaching'? 32

What strategies are there for coping with problems of communication? 34

How can I incorporate differentiation and personalisation? 35

Cross-curricular links 37

Intercultural understanding 38

Assessment 39

Self-assessment 40

Summary 41

Contents

Part 2 How good does my French have to be?   42

Combating feeling rusty   42

Worrying about your accent   42

Making mistakes   42

Conducting lessons in French   42

Worrying about grammar   43

Classroom language   43

Pupil language   47

Part 3 Sample units and lesson plans   48

How to use these lessons   48

Unit 1: Numbers   50

Unit 2: Colours   60

Unit 3: Parts of the body   70

Part 4 Photocopiable pages   78

Loto   78

Les nombres   79

Dix euros (chanson)   80

Découvre le numéro !   81

Calculs   82

Mots croisés (1)   83

Jeu   84

Jeu des couleurs   85

Mots croisés (2)   86

Colorie l'image   87

Le corps   88

Rap (chanson)   89

Un robot et un monstre   90

Qu'est-ce qui manque ?   91

Part 5 Key factors for success   92

How to build a solid foundation   92

How to keep your teaching fresh and stimulating   93

Recommended further reading   94

Resources on the CD-ROM

Interactive activities

Unit 1: Numbers

Activité 1. Clique, écoute et répète.

Activité 2. Ecoute et clique.

Activité 3. Dix euros (chanson).

Activité 4. Ecoute et clique sur le nombre.

Unit 2: Colours

Activité 5. Clique, écoute et regarde.

Activité 6. Ecoute et clique.

Activité 7. Qu'est-ce qui manque ?

Activité 8. Trouve la couleur.

Activité 9. Trouve un poisson.

Unit 3: Parts of the body

Activité 10. Clique, écoute et répète.

Activité 11. Rap : un, deux … (chanson).

Activité12. Ecoute et colorie le clown.

Activité 13. Fais un bonhomme de neige.

Photocopiable pages

Loto

Les nombres

Dix euros (chanson)

Découvre le numéro !

Calculs

Mots croisés (1)

Jeu

Jeu des couleurs

Mots croisés (2)

Colorie l'image

Le corps

Rap (chanson)

Un robot et un monstre

Qu'est-ce qui manque ?

Flashcards

1. Rouge
2. Blanc
3. Bleu
4. Vert
5. Jaune
6. Noir
7. Rose
8. Orange
9. Gris
10. Brun
11. Violet
12. Drapeau

Audio tracks

1. Un, deux, trois …
2. Dix, neuf, huit …
3. Dix euros (chanson)
4. Jeu des couleurs
5. Quelle est ta couleur préférée ?
6. Rime : la tête, les oreilles …
7. Rap : un, deux … (chanson)

How to use the CD-ROM

System requirements

Minimum specifications:

- PC or Mac with CD-ROM drive and at least 512 MB of RAM (recommended);
- Windows 2000 or XP/ Mac OSX.2 or above;
- 1024 x 768 minimum screen resolution;
- 16 bit sound and 3D graphics card.

Navigation

The CD-ROM that accompanies this book includes a range of resources to support both the teacher's own French and the lessons in this book. The **main interface** links to the different types of resources: classroom language; interactive activities; worksheets; flashcards and audio.

Classroom language

This section is designed to support the teacher's use of French in the classroom and provides, in both audio and written form, a fund of words and phrases essential for conducting lessons.

Click on a phrase to hear the correct pronunciation.

Click **Show/Hide** to hide or reveal the French or the English text.

Test yourself by:

- hiding the English, then playing a piece of audio to see whether you can give its meaning.
- showing just the English and providing the French, checking it by hearing or reading the French – or both.

By ticking any combination of topics on the index page, then selecting **Test yourself**, you can assess your knowledge of a random selection of phrases taken from those topics.

Interactive activities

These are divided by unit, according to the teaching units within this book. Interactive activities take the form of:

- Presentation of new vocabulary;
- Games for the children to play;
- Songs with 'karaoke' text.

Each unit has four or five interactive activities, which should be used in conjunction with the lessons outlined in this book. Note that the sound buttons are not relevant for all the interactives and will therefore only function during certain activities.

Worksheets

The worksheets printed in this book are also available to be printed directly from this CD-ROM. Selecting **Worksheets** from the main interface opens a new window where the worksheets are listed as PDF files. In order to view and print these you will therefore need Adobe® Acrobat® Reader® installed on your computer.

Flashcards

The 'Colours' unit in the book includes reference to 12 flashcards, which have been provided on the CD-ROM (11 colours and the French flag). As above, selecting **Flashcards** from the main interface opens a new window where they are listed as PDF files. You will need Adobe® Acrobat® Reader® installed on your computer in order to view and print these.

Audio files

Select **Audio** from the main interface in order to select and play the audio tracks referred to in the lesson plans in this book.

Using this CD-ROM with other programs

To switch between the CD-ROM and other programs on your computer, hold down the 'alt' key on your keyboard and the press 'tab'.

Technical support

For all technical support queries, please contact Scholastic Customer Services on 0845 603 9091.

Introduction

To rephrase a famous quote: some people are born French, some people achieve French and some people have French thrust upon them. Whichever category you belong to, here are a number of considerations which should reassure you:

- Younger children take to languages like ducks to water.
- Language teaching can easily be made both varied and fun.
- Feedback about language learning in primary schools (worldwide) is overwhelmingly positive.
- There are good structures and resources in place which can support you: you won't have to figure it all out for yourself.

This book is designed to give you the understanding and the confidence you will need to go into your classroom and teach French. In the knowledge that primary teachers are busy people and that French is only one of many subjects they have to teach, it only goes into as much theory as is necessary to deal with the real issues of teaching in the classroom. It not only gives advice and tips but also provides teaching materials – resources to print (photocopiable worksheets and flashcards) as well as audio and interactive software – based on the acclaimed *Petit Pont,* to help you get started.

Many teachers feel understandably nervous about trying to teach a language they themselves are not specialists in. Yet primary teachers have to teach a whole range of subjects that are not their speciality. So what is it about teaching a language that tends to make people feel so nervous? This and other issues about using French in the classroom are dealt with in the next chapter: 'What do I need to know about language teaching?' In addition, the CD-ROM includes a section designed specifically to support and develop your use of French in the classroom. (The contents of resources both in the book and on the CD-ROM are listed on page 5.)

Why teach a foreign language?

The fact that you are reading this probably means you are at least partly convinced of the value of children starting a foreign language at a young age. Learning a foreign language is already the norm in many countries throughout the world and is soon to become a statutory requirement in England and Wales. But let us try to remove any doubts by considering the arguments in its favour.

- Not only a significant body of research but, more importantly, the personal experience of thousands of teachers, attest to the beneficial effects of language learning for children's cognitive development. It develops a flexibility of thinking and enhances their problem-solving skills. It is, if you like, a form of mental gymnastics. Any teacher embarking on teaching a foreign language cannot fail to be aware of the mental muscles of their own that are about to be flexed!

- It reinforces children's first language development: through comparison, it illuminates their understanding of their own language. As Goethe said: 'He who doesn't know a foreign language cannot know his own' (*Maximen und Reflexionen*).

- Learning a foreign language not only helps children with development of their native language: learning that first foreign language equips them with the techniques for learning other languages later in life.

- It is a pleasure to be able to communicate (at any level) in another language. It opens up possibilities for more rewarding travel and it is an unquestionably useful skill in many fields of work.

- Learning a new language is the ideal means of developing an understanding of another culture and thereby of other cultures in general. It helps to create an appreciation of what we have in common with, and a tolerance for what is different about, other cultures.

- It is fun!

Why French?

For mainly historical reasons, French is the predominant foreign language taught in the UK: France is our nearest neighbour and the majority of teachers themselves learned French at school. There are strong arguments for teaching other languages and some, such as Chinese and Polish, are growing in popularity. However, one of the challenges in education is providing continuity.

Although there is an argument for introducing children to different languages at different stages of their schooling, it is common and natural for teachers, parents and pupils to feel that they want to ensure the possibility of progress in whatever language children start and to learn a language at primary school only to find you cannot pursue it at secondary level is bound to be frustrating. For this reason, some authorities have deliberately chosen – even if with reservations – to teach at primary a language that children can be guaranteed to continue at secondary. For better or worse, this tends to be French.

What do I have to teach?

Schemes of work and the Key Stage 2 Framework for Languages

The QCA *Scheme of Work for French*, though non-statutory, identifies the topics and the language that should be covered at Key Stage 2. It proposes a sequence of activities for each topic but acknowledges that teachers may want to vary the order and manner in which these topics are covered throughout the key stage. Different published materials take advantage of the flexibility offered by QCA and the Framework to structure the content in different ways. These (like the resources provided with this book) have the advantage of providing appropriate and attractive resources to support you each step of the way.

A scheme of work needs to identify:

- the topics to be covered;
- the actual language associated with each of these topics;
- the resources available for teaching them.

If you do not have a scheme of work in place, don't panic. There are models available both in local authorities and commercially which will save you hours of work. What is the point of everyone devising their own individual schemes of work from scratch, when so much can be gained from sharing experience and skills with others who have already spent years thinking about it? Good course materials too will be based on an analysis of the required content and will have sequenced it to ensure a logical progression.

In secondary language teaching the majority of schools allow a published course to provide this map for them. In primary, where teachers are more in the habit of picking and choosing from a range of resources, a good scheme of work becomes more important. But no scheme of work should be set in stone: it can and should be modified and developed over time.

The *Key Stage 2 Framework for Languages* is more about *how* to teach than *what* to teach. It does not prescribe topics or list vocabulary and grammar to teach. Instead, it identifies what it calls the five 'strands' to language teaching and proposes ways that these should be developed. These strands are:

- Oracy: developing the skills of listening and speaking;
- Literacy: developing the skills of reading and writing;
- Intercultural understanding: in which the language is seen as a door to a wider appreciation of the culture as a whole;
- Knowledge about language: becoming aware of the nature and characteristics of the language (and of language in general);
- Language learning strategies: becoming aware of techniques and procedures of how to learn.

Taking these five 'strands' as the essential tasks of language learning, the Framework suggests how they should be woven into your teaching throughout the four years over which MFL is notionally taught in primary schools. It is important to keep in mind that it is not a substitute for a scheme of work, which is the road map you need to follow from week to week and from term to term.

You may hear people talking about 'delivering the Framework'. This is putting the cart before the horse. The Framework should be seen as a guide and a support – not as the master to be served.

Choosing resources and materials

Though printed materials, sound recordings and interactive software are only a part of what you will be using in your classroom during French lessons, they are an important part. Obviously, word of mouth and recommendations from colleagues will play a central role in your choice. Here are a few key considerations to take into account:

- Does it provide a variety of activity type? Is there enough material to keep you going?
- Does it incorporate (for example, in a teacher's guide) suggestions for activities and games apart from those directly dependent on the materials?
- Are there things for children to work on in their own time?
- Does it convey a feeling of France and things French? Most children will probably not have been to France, so to give them a flavour of the country is important.
- If it is a supplementary resource, does it match the other resources you are using in terms of vocabulary and level of difficulty?
- If it includes recorded speech, is it clear and not too fast?
- Is it good value for money?

An extensive list of language-teaching resources and publishers can be found on the NACELL website (National Advisory Centre for Early Language Learning): www.nacell.org.uk/resources/publishers.htm

Lots of useful advice and ideas can also be found in the excellent *Young Pathfinder* series published by CILT. Also see the list of resources in this book provided on page 94.

What do I need to know about language teaching?

Views about the best way to teach languages change almost as fast as designer fashions! Over the last quarter of a century attitudes towards the teaching of grammar, the use of French only in the classroom, the role of reading and writing, and many other things have swung from one extreme to the other. Those that are preached today will change too. But there are certain fundamental issues about which there is now broad agreement and these will be discussed in this section.

How long and how often?

Several shorter sessions a week are better than one long one. 'Little and often' is more likely to build up children's knowledge and confidence. So how little is little? Even a fifteen-minute session is enough to make real progress: two of these a week will be more effective than one single session of 30 minutes. Of course, if at all possible, it would be better to spend more than just half an hour a week on French, but if that's as much as you can squeeze in, it is still absolutely worthwhile.

If, in addition to whole-class lessons, children have the opportunity to spend time on computers (in school or at home) using appropriate interactive software, this is an excellent way of reinforcing what you have done together.

Many teachers find that, once French has become popular, they can use it as a reward: a short game or song at the end of a session for example (see pages 50–77 for ideas). If you are teaching French to your regular class, there are plenty of opportunities for incorporating bits of French into the school day.

How to... use French throughout the school day

You can take the register in French, expecting children to reply *Oui* or *absent* (if it's a girl, it will be *absente*).

Say *Bonjour* or *Ça va ?* (How are you?) to each child, requiring them to answer in French:

Bonjour, James.

Bonjour, Mademoiselle.

Bonjour, Laura. Ça va ?

Ça va.

You can reuse common expressions and instructions in other curriculum areas, for example in PE lessons or giving instructions when going to and from assembly. (See the next chapter – 'How good does my French have to be?' – or the 'Classroom language' section on the CD-ROM for examples.)

How do I provide enough practice?

For the vast majority of learners it is essential to get plenty of practice at any new vocabulary or grammar, so that it really takes root. Therefore, the first big challenge for teachers is: how to provide enough practice to ensure that children really get to grips with new material without it becoming boring.

New words have to be heard and said many times before they really stick. For some learners, reading and even writing them will help the learning process (see page 27). The key to providing a lot of practice is to make it varied and engaging. Using a variety of flashcard games and – if you have an interactive whiteboard available – interactive games is usually the best means. Some examples of games you can play with flashcards can be found on page 62. Samples of interactive games are provided on the CD-ROM accompanying this book.

Remember:

It is also important that you choose the right amount of new material to introduce. Children who can manage six new words or phrases at a time may end up remembering nothing if you try to teach them twelve. But there is no right answer to how many new words at a time you should introduce. This will depend on the aptitude of the children as well as on the difficulty of the words themselves.

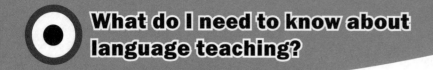

How do I recycle material?

Once new material has taken root, it needs to be kept alive. Words and phrases need to be recycled otherwise there is a serious risk that children will simply forget them. Therefore, the second challenge is: how to recycle this material often enough without children complaining, 'We've done this before'.

Variety is the key to recycling topics and language that have been learned before. We do not generally get up in the morning and say, 'Oh no! Not breakfast! I had that yesterday!' There is no inherent reason why revisiting a topic should be unwelcome as long as it can be made interesting or enjoyable.

To achieve the desired variety of activities with the quality of graphics and recorded sound necessary to keep children's interest, you will inevitably need to use some published materials. Some schools, regional groups and local authorities produce excellent materials of their own, and it is true that there is some satisfaction to be gained from working with resources you have produced yourself with particular classes in mind. However, it is very time consuming to produce all your own material and it is virtually impossible to produce interactive material of a commercial standard. Your time is much better spent planning what activities to do, selecting materials, games, worksheets or websites and ensuring that you are confident with the language you will need to deliver the lesson effectively.

In addition to whatever commercial materials you decide to use, take every opportunity to share ideas with colleagues, make the most of regional support groups, internet forums, and any in-service training available.

How can I improve pronunciation?

It is curious that most of us, while developing our knowledge of a foreign language, somehow fail to improve our accent or our pronunciation. Though children are more open to imitation and have a better ear, they too will stop trying to improve their pronunciation very much unless consciously encouraged to do so. Do not assume that making the right noises is something that only needs to be practised at the beginning. Regularly spend a few minutes on the pronunciation of a key sound that the children have heard recently, or with which they have difficulty.

Intonation is inextricably linked with pronunciation. The pitch and rhythm of the words in a sentence are as important as the sounds in individual words. Encourage children to hear and imitate the intonation of real French speakers. One key characteristic of French which is never given enough attention is the fact that, unlike most languages, it doesn't place the stress on one particular syllable of a word, but rather every syllable is stressed equally.

How to... improve pronunciation

Groups of children can be asked to practise a sound together, then put forward who they agree is pronouncing it best. This will help them to concentrate on the sounds without forcing anyone to perform poorly in public.

How to... hear the difference between French and English

Listen to the French and English pronunciation of cognates such as

café

restaurant

omelette

gâteau

In English, the stress in these words is on the first syllable; in French, all the syllables carry equal weight. This, more than any particular sounds, is what gives French its distinctive quality. Getting children to grasp this, and to practise it, will help them to sound more French.

Don't worry if your own accent is less than perfect. Indeed, unless you grow up completely bilingual, it is virtually impossible to have a perfect accent. Make no apologies for using audio recordings or interactive software as a model for pronunciation.

How can I develop communication?

One tendency in teaching beginners is simply to teach a set of words relating to each topic – family, pets, colours and so on – because there are lots of games that can be played to make this fun. So what is the problem with this? There is nothing wrong with teaching by topics: children themselves like this and there is convincing research in favour of its effectiveness. The danger is that they will end up knowing a set of nouns which they can use to name things, but that they won't be able to get beyond this to any real level of communication.

Without verbs (and pronouns) you can't get very far. But 'verbs' in this sense doesn't mean action words like 'play', 'jump' or 'swim'. The most useful verbs in any language are ones such as 'have' (*avoir*), 'go' (*aller*), 'be' (*être*) or 'like' (*aimer*). These have the disadvantage that you can't illustrate them with a colourful picture, label them, or point to them, but they are the key building blocks of communication and it is essential that they are introduced and reused consistently from the start. The best way to avoid the dangers of simply word learning is to use materials which take this into account and build whole-sentence use into their progression. You will find examples of this in the sample materials that form part of this package.

Vocabulary learning, however, does have its place. When embarking on a new topic, it is perfectly natural to introduce a new set of vocabulary. It is also essential to practise it in a number of ways to help children become familiar and confident with it, before asking them to combine it with other words or use it in any more complicated ways. But equally, it is important not to leave it at this. To ensure you are not just teaching lists of words, always ask yourself: what things do I want them to be able to say when they have completed this topic? These are as likely to be questions as they are answers or statements.

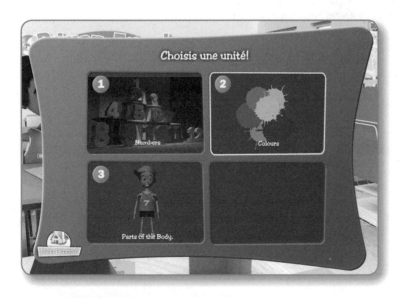

How to... introduce questions

Imagine you have just taught the colours. This is an enjoyable topic, offering lots of opportunities for fun and games, but what practical use can it be put to? Depending on what vocabulary the children have learned previously, they could ask each other:

- *De quelle couleur est ta chambre ?* (What colour is your bedroom?)
- *De quelle couleur est ta maison ?* (What colour is your house?) ... *ta voiture ?* (...your car?) ...*ton sac ?* (...your bag?) ... *ton t-shirt préféré ?* (...your favourite t-shirt?)
- *Quelle est ta couleur préférée ?* (What is your favourite colour?

Suppose you have taught the days of the week. Teach the question:

- *On est quel jour ?* (What day is it?)

This can legitimately be asked in class every day.

If you have already taught the words for any sports or spare-time activities, combine these with the days of the week:

- *Sam, tu joues au foot ? Quels jours ?* (Sam, day you play football? What days?)
- If Sam doesn't understand, prompt with: *vendredi,* (Friday), *samedi* (Saturday)?

Setting new vocabulary in a realistic context like this will help to convince children of the point of learning the language.

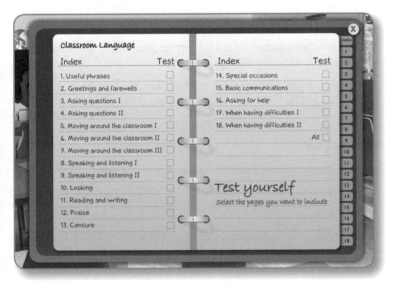

How do I encourage children to ask and answer questions?

It is a natural tendency in a classroom for the teacher to ask questions and the children to answer them. In foreign language learning, though, it is as important to be able to formulate the questions as to give an answer. Besides, there is no better way of becoming familiar with language of any kind than actually using it yourself, as opposed to just hearing it. So get children asking as well as answering.

How to... play question games

● Play chain games where child A asks child B a given question, such as *Quel âge as-tu ?* (How old are you?) Child B answers it, *J'ai huit ans* (I'm eight), then turns to child C and asks them the same question, and so on.

This can be played as a single chain right round the class, or in teams, in which case an element of competition can be introduced.

● Play games that involve children asking each other questions.

● Give an answer and ask children to work out what the question was. For example:

Voici une réponse : 'Je m'appelle Mathieu'. Quelle est la question ? (Here is an answer: 'My name is Matthew'. What's the question?)

Comment tu t'appelles ? (What's your name?)

Oui. Bien.

● When the children have learned a bit more French, you can repeat the exercise above in a more open-ended way:

Voici une réponse: 'Oui ! C'est super !' Quelle est la question ? (Here is an answer: 'Yes! It's super!' What's the question?)

Tu aimes le chocolat ? (Do you like chocolate?) or *Regarde mon T-shirt !* (Look at my T-shirt!)

There are a number of possibilities here. Children can be encouraged to think up as many as they can.

There is a tradition in some quarters, left over from answering written exam questions, to require learners to answer questions with whole sentences. However, in conversation it is far better to be natural. Who, if asked, 'What's your dog's name?' would answer, 'My dog's name is…'? Nobody. We would simply say the name.

How important is learning by heart?

Vocabulary has to be learned word by word. Grammar, in contrast, far from being the forbidding part of language learning, should be seen as the merciful exception to this brick-by-brick approach. Grammar allows you to short-circuit all this rote learning and to predict and work out what certain words are going (or at least, are likely) to do.

The value of learning certain patterns by heart is that it saves you having to think about them. How many times have you heard (or said), 'When I'm actually there, talking French, I just can't think of the words fast enough'? Learning key patterns by heart goes some way towards overcoming this. Besides, since when did young children hate learning things by heart?

How to... encourage learning by heart

● Play games that make children realise the convenience of knowing things by heart, rather than having to rummage through their memories for them. Of course, it is essential not to overdo it. Judging just how much and how often you ask children to memorise things is crucial.

● Learn the alphabet. Some people object to teaching the French alphabet on the grounds that it is an artificial activity you'll never use and that it may cause confusion with the English alphabet if children have only recently learned that. Both my own experience and that of observing many other classes is that children love learning it. This is probably because – in contrast to most vocabulary learning – it is such a satisfyingly self-contained task. It is not **an** alphabet: it is **the** alphabet. And when you know it, you'll know it for ever. But it is also an excellent way to focus on the basic French sounds without worrying about meaning. If you are not sure of the French alphabet, it is can be heard on page 11 of the 'Classroom language' section of the CD-ROM.

How should I use French in the classroom?

When teaching French, it is generally accepted that it is best to stay in the 'target language' as much as possible. In other words, don't keep reverting to English to give instructions, to praise children or to tell them off. There are good reasons for this:

- It convinces children that this new language is a genuine means of communication: you really can use it for ordinary purposes instead of English. While they are aware that when asking their way to the shop in class they are only pretending, using French to ask permission to go to the toilet can achieve real results.

- While you will be concentrating on different topic areas at different times in your French teaching (numbers, colours, pets and so on) you will be using classroom instructions and praise in every lesson. Children will therefore have the opportunity to become familiar with these expressions quite naturally, without you having to contrive situations or activities to introduce them.

But teaching in the 'target language' is easier said than done. So what are the challenges – particularly for the non-specialist teacher – in using French for classroom-management purposes?

- The are terms you will probably not have used before, being so specific to the task of teaching. You will therefore have to learn and practise it so it becomes second nature to you in the classroom. This is not as daunting as it sounds. Even if you knew them all, you wouldn't be able to use them all straight away since children wouldn't understand them. Set yourself a few each week to introduce and use regularly in class.

- *Tu* and *vous*: the two words for 'you'. Switching between the singular form *tu* (when you are talking to one child) and the plural *vous* (when you are talking to several or to the whole class) is one of the most difficult things a teacher has to cope with. Unless your French is excellent, you will make mistakes with this. Don't worry. It will come with practice. The list of classroom language gives both the singular and the plural form of all instructions. Fortunately, in most cases the two are very similar. And besides, few children will notice if you get them wrong from time to time.

- It is not only you who will need to learn special phrases for use in class. The children too should learn how to ask for a pencil in French, to ask you to repeat something, and so on. In what other school situation, when asked a question, could a pupil expect to earn praise for correctly saying, 'I don't know'?

- It is a good idea to produce a few simple posters to illustrate basic instructions ('sit down!'; 'be quiet!'; 'hands up!') and display them in your classroom. You could get the children to make them themselves: photos taken in class could be used to illustrate them.

The 'Classroom language' section of the CD-ROM offers help with all these points. The following chapter of this book also includes a full list of key language for use in the classroom.

Remember:

All this classroom language is not just a means to carry out learning: it is an important part of the learning itself. If you reach the point where you are effectively managing the lesson in French, this represents a great achievement in itself for both you and the children!

Is grammar important?

When we learn our own language we do it without reference to rules of any kind. This doesn't mean our mind isn't constructing rules for itself: look at the way small children will form false past tenses like 'builded' or 'hurted'. This can only be because they have recognised a pattern in verbs they have heard and applied it to others. But we are not conscious of the workings of our own language. When we reach a certain level of confidence in another language, these conscious mechanisms gradually become habits and eventually become instinctive. Anyone who has become proficient at another language will remember that satisfying feeling when they realised that words were coming to them 'without having to think about it'. This is the fundamental process we are trying to achieve when learning a new language:

conscious understanding   instinct

$\longrightarrow$

Grammar is nothing but a short cut to describing the workings of a language. For a whole generation, it was considered to be something that would 'put children off'. All mention of it was avoided in textbooks. Helpful explanations of the habits of verbs, nouns, adjectives and so on were shunned for fear that the mere mention of these terms might alienate or confuse learners. It was as if you were teaching someone to drive but were not allowed to use words like 'brake', 'accelerator' or 'steering wheel'. This grammarphobia was itself a reaction against the kind of grammar-based teaching that had left a previous generation able to translate Molière but unable to ask the way to the station. Fortunately, this folly is now behind us and children now learn basic grammatical terminology and concepts in literacy. Much of what the KS2 Framework refers to as 'Knowledge about language' is simply grammar under another name. But it remains an area that has to be trodden with care.

How should the teaching of grammar be approached?

Encourage children to think in terms of patterns rather than rules. The term 'rule' automatically brings with it an expectation that it will be followed. The immediate discovery – which invariably occurs with any language – that there are numerous exceptions, is bound to be discouraging if not exasperating. What's more, when you discover that it is the commonest words, the most important players, which totally disregard the rules, it is natural for learners to wonder what is the point of them. Imagine if that happened in a sport!

It is important not only for children to think in terms of language patterns, but also for them to have the chance to discover these for themselves. Think of it as a scientific experiment: it is much more motivating to observe and try to work out what is happening for yourself than to have someone else simply explain it all to you.

How to... approach grammar

When dealing with grammar, try to apply the following precepts:

● Allow children to see or hear the new language and to use it themselves.

● Encourage them to observe what is happening in the language and to try to spot the pattern.

● Clarify and explain the pattern yourself, with examples, starting from their own observations.

● Provide them with opportunities to use the language again, equipped with the new, more conscious knowledge of how it works.

Exploring language patterns is the most constructive way of viewing grammar. But more often than not, people think of grammar as being all about accuracy: Are you getting the endings right? Are you making mistakes? In a learner's mind, the obvious question is: does it matter if I get things wrong? Whether it matters can only be judged against what you are hoping to achieve. If you are aiming to be able to communicate and understand the language at a basic level, then clearly some mistakes are more serious than others. Failing to make adjectives agree or making a masculine noun feminine never stopped a foreigner understanding anyone! However, misuse of verbs can lead to serious misunderstanding: telling someone that you have eaten when what you mean is that you want to eat could have very disagreeable consequences. With this in mind, it is important to judge how much emphasis to place on different aspects of grammar. If children perceive that you are making a fuss about details, they will naturally tend to lose interest. In any case, a balance has to be achieved between communication and accuracy.

Genders

When starting to learn French, children will probably be coming across the phenomenon of gender for the first time: they will discover that in French all things animate and inanimate are either masculine or feminine. This is a very strange idea to a native English speaker and it is natural to ask why. What is the point of it? How can you possibly know whether a towel is masculine or feminine? Without trying to justify it, this can be presented in a positive light. It's like going abroad: you would hope that people's natural curiosity would lead them to be interested in what is different about a foreign country and not dismissive just because things are not what they are used to. In the same way what is different about another language is partly what makes it interesting. At all costs you need to discourage children from thinking of it as a 'nuisance' that other languages do not do things the way English does.

Do not be afraid to ask children to learn the *le* and *la* for a new group of words. This is a fundamental part of the language so don't be apologetic about it: do you keep apologising for English spelling? Instead find enjoyable ways of learning genders and checking whether the children have remembered them correctly.

Verb endings

Compared to English's very simple verb endings (I like, you like, we like, they like and so on), those of French can appear daunting. One of the problems is that you can't hear lots of the differences. *Je mange* sounds the same as *tu manges*, which sounds the same as *ils* or *elles mangent*. Look on the bright side: if you are focusing on the spoken forms, children can learn these as a single form. But what happens when you come to the written forms? The problem is the same for young French children who grow up hearing them as one sound, then discover that they are spelled in different ways. French primary children get tested exhaustively on the spellings of verbs on the principle that nothing but rote learning can equip them with the necessary bank of knowledge. This would clearly not work for young British learners but certain models or 'paradigms' of how verbs behave are as useful as they are unfashionable. For example:

Je vais	*Nous allons*
Tu vas	*Vous allez*
Il va	*Ils vont*

For more information on learning by heart see page 19.

Tu and *vous*

Most European languages have more than one word for 'you'. English, of course, used to be the same (thee, thou, ye, you) – as it is worth pointing out to pupils – but its use declined until it is now barely heard outside wedding ceremonies and the Lord's Prayer. In French the problem is compounded by the fact that *vous* serves two purposes: it is the plural form whoever you're talking to and it is the polite form if you're only talking to one person.

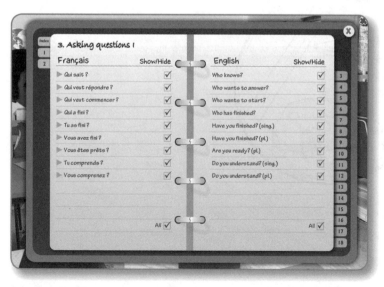

As a teacher, you have to remember to use *tu* when talking to one child and *vous* when addressing a pair or a group of children, or the whole class. It is a difficult habit to get used to and comes with the additional challenge of finding the correct verb form to go with each (*tu comprends ? vous comprenez ?*). Do not despair. The actual number of phrases you will need to use in class is more limited than you might think. Help with practising these is available in the 'Classroom language' section of the accompanying CD-ROM.

In the classroom you will be using both *tu* and *vous*. This means that children will hear both on a regular basis. The conversations they will be having with each other, in contrast, will always use *tu*. To what extent should you try to explain this? As with any of the more difficult grammatical issues, the best advice is: let them hear it and get used to it long before you attempt a formal explanation of what's going on. Ideally, wait until they themselves ask for an explanation.

Tenses

In real life we tend to talk about the past and the future: what we did or what we're going to do. People can see what we're actually doing, so unless we're on the mobile ('I'm on the train') we tend not to describe it. We move freely between talking about the past, the present and the future. In my own view it is therefore a pity that we keep children operating in the prison of the present tense for so long. This is the legacy of old academic traditions which analysed grammar and then built a syllabus on that basis with little regard to what it would be useful to know.

It is in the handling of tenses that almost everyone who has learned French at school feels particularly inept when confronted with the real language. How ironic that the so-called perfect tense ends up being so far from perfect with most of us. But in spite of this, the habit of starting and staying in the present persists. Be aware of this in your teaching and do not be afraid to teach key phrases like: *J'ai fini* (I've finished); *Je vais ouvrir la fenêtre* (I'm going to open the window). In this way, without explicitly referring to the names of tenses, children will become familiar with key patterns.

So why bother with accuracy at all?

It is true that some people – we have all met them – manage to communicate perfectly well in a foreign language although what they say may be riddled with mistakes. It is also true that most people who aspire to learn another language would be very happy if they could just communicate in it. But it is equally true that most of us, when we start to develop an interest in something – whether it's a sport, a hobby or a work-related skill – tend to want to make a certain amount of progress. We may not have any delusions about becoming experts in it, but we generally like to achieve a high enough standard in order to be able to take part reasonably effectively.

The balance between encouragement and correction

One of the skills of a good language teacher is to be able to strike a balance between giving pupils encouragement for their progress and pointing out things that can be improved. Take opportunities to praise them for their accuracy when you are not particularly focusing on that. If they communicate their message inaccurately but effectively, build onto your praise for their communication a discreet correction to the detail. Just how much you correct and how often is a matter for your professional judgement. Some children will react more positively than others. We can all remember how discouraging a page covered in red ink can be.

In any case, you will not be doing children any favours by ignoring all the errors. It is annoying, after someone has been telling you that everything's fine, to discover at a later date that you have been getting things wrong. Because language learning is so much about habit forming, overlooking significant errors is in fact only helping them to form bad habits. These will be much harder to unlearn later.

As far as marking goes, the following pictorial code is one I have found effective. It relates accuracy to communication.

 message clearly communicated

 message clear in spite of some inaccuracies

 message partly obscured by inaccuracies

 bits of the message get through

 message doesn't get through

To avoid the need for doing little drawings every time (though children like that) these symbols can be labelled A, B, C, D and E and work can then be graded using a letter. The code can be displayed in the classroom or each child can keep a copy of it in their book.

At what point should reading and writing be introduced?

At what point you introduce the written word will depend primarily on the age of the children. Younger children who have only recently started to read and write will naturally gain less from it than those who have already acquired these basic skills in their own language. However, there is no right answer to this question. Let us consider the arguments.

Will seeing French letter strings be confusing?

Much is said about the dangers of introducing reading and writing into early foreign-language learning. The arguments generally revolve around the claim that children will tend to decode a written French word according to the phonic rules they are familiar with and so mispronounce it, whereas if they only heard the word they would be more likely to retain the correct pronunciation. This is the 'silver plate' (*s'il vous plaît*) argument.

It's true that sometimes a child will get it wrong, but most children are perfectly capable of realising that the sound-spelling relationships are different in another language. To see the word *château*, even if they are not familiar with the sound made by the letter string *eau*, can nonetheless help many learners to 'picture' the word and thus to remember it. This does not, of course, mean they should be expected to remember the spelling.

It is a fact that many if not most people (children no less than adults) find it difficult to disentangle the individual words when they hear spoken French. Even oral repetition does not necessarily help. If you yourself have found it helpful to see a written version of something you've heard – even if you have no desire to learn the spelling – then why should we assume that children will be any different?

(This is not to say there may not be certain children for whom it is unhelpful, and it is obviously important to be alert to these. You do not want to put a child who is struggling with literacy off French by doubling their burden.)

It is also important to recognise that developing literacy skills in French will in turn contribute to literacy in English. Together, they will reinforce children's phonic awareness.

chat   château

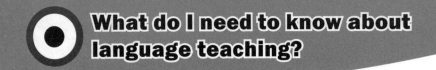

Will reading and writing be too much like hard work?

Another argument sometimes used against the introduction of reading and writing is that it makes the lessons less fun – more like 'work'. Surely it is important, with language becoming a permanent part of the primary curriculum, that it be seen as just as serious a subject as any other. It is not in its long-term interest that French be thought of as all fun and games.

Finally, there is one fairly obvious way (one that surprisingly few 'experts' refer to) of ascertaining whether seeing the written word in the foreign language helps or hinders children: ask them!

The four skills

Most activities in a language lesson involve a combination of two or more of the four skills: it's almost impossible (and certainly not an endearing quality) to converse with someone without listening; writing tasks almost always involve reading; feedback to listening or reading activities is normally in spoken or written form; and reading or writing is often used to support speaking. Do not waste time trying to break down every task into its component skills: the fact that they are divided into the strands of oracy and literacy in the KS2 Framework in no way implies that they need to be separated out in practice.

Receptive and productive skills

This is a useful distinction to bear in mind. Listening and reading are described as receptive skills. That's to say, you are trying to understand something, not to express anything. Speaking and writing, on the other hand, are referred to as productive skills.

It is worth ensuring that in the early phases of any new topic you concentrate on receptive skills. Learners need to absorb the material before being asked to do something with it. If you move too quickly on to productive tasks, it can undermine children's confidence. Concrete examples of this principle can be found in the proposed sequences of activities later on in this book.

Using stories

It is not just enjoyment that stories can introduce to language teaching. Aspects of French culture – festivals, traditions and just details of daily life – become much more interesting when part of a story than when delivered as raw, cultural information. Also, more than any other device, stories offer the potential for children to be able to understand a sustained piece of French.

It is natural for a teacher to be concerned, however, that the text, whether spoken or read, may be too long or demanding for children to follow.

Many teachers would rather avoid an experiment that may damage children's carefully built confidence, but there are ways of safeguarding against this.

How to... use stories successfully

● It is important to realise that children do not need to understand every word of a story to be able to follow its general meaning. Indeed, in learning any foreign language, one of the absolute certainties is that you will never be able to understand everything.

● Using illustrations goes a long way to supporting understanding, pointing at details of the pictures to explain the meaning.

● Using a story that children already know has the advantage of helping them to guess at the meanings of new words and phrases, particularly if it is one in which key expressions are repeated ('And they pulled, and they pulled, and they pulled'; 'What big teeth you've got, grandma!' and so on).

● Of course, it's possible to spend time teaching new vocabulary that occurs in the story and it's worth learning the French for 'giant turnip', for example, in order to enjoy that traditional tale even if you're unlikely to find much use for it in everyday life. But to take a lot of time out from the core language you want children to learn, just in order to be able to understand one story, is probably inappropriate.

Certain well-known picture books lend themselves well to being told in French, though authentic French versions sometimes contain language that is very idiomatic or unusual, and writing a French version of your own requires a high level of competence. An alternative is to use a resource in which the stories have been written specifically to reflect and reinforce the language children have been learning. They can then enjoy them without the need for extensive preparation and have the satisfaction of ready understanding.

Let us come back to an earlier question: should children read or just hear the story? On the one hand, seeing at least key phrases can often help them to 'get hold' of the meaning – especially if they contain familiar vocabulary. On the other hand, there is a tremendous satisfaction to be gained from understanding a story that you are simply told. The experience somehow confirms that you have really tuned in to the language and that you can understand it, as it were, without props. This will only work, though, if the story is one they are already familiar with or if it is firmly constructed out of language they already know.

Using songs

No teacher who has ever used songs needs convincing of their effectiveness or of their appeal. Here are just a few of the advantages they can offer in language teaching:

- Songs involve active participation. Many can be accompanied by actions.
- The rhythm and the rhyme of songs naturally focus children's attention on the sounds of the language, encouraging them to imitate what they hear.
- Songs are a great way to get everybody to join in.

- Where repeating a phrase over and over can easily seem pointless and become boring, it is perfectly acceptable in the context of a song and can be positively fun.

- For some reason we tend to remember language from rhymes and songs better than anything else: things we learned in the nursery often stay with us all our life.

- Whereas in a conversation or printed text we would find it frustrating to meet things we don't understand, this doesn't seem to matter so much in a song. Children even sing bits of songs in their own language whose meaning they're not sure about! Full understanding is not a requirement; difficult bits are not a barrier.

Should the songs be authentic or traditional?

It is nice for children to learn one or two songs that they know are sung by French children and which, in that sense, are 'real'. 'Frère Jacques' and 'Sur le pont d'Avignon' are a safe bet. The fact is, however, that the language of many authentic songs will pose a real challenge to beginners. You therefore need to weigh up authenticity against manageability. A specially written song which highlights the language you have been teaching has a lot to be said for it. The key thing to ask about it – assuming the French is correct – is quite simply: do the children like it? (Two songs are included on the CD-ROM which accompanies this book.)

Finally, remember that children may be learning a new tune as well as dealing with a foreign language. Allow them to join in in their own time – and at their own volume!

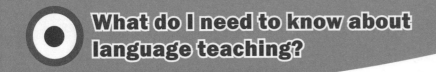

What is 'communicative language teaching'?

The word 'communicative' is bandied about in the world of modern languages as if everyone knows what it means. It seems to carry a great deal of weight, but in reality it's a very vague term. Don't be put off by it.

Communicative language teaching in its broadest sense was a reaction to the approach which taught grammar and vocabulary without any real sense of its practical purpose. One of the early phrases in the book I used to improve my Spanish was: 'This is the surgeon who amputated my brother's arm.' One of the first phrases I ever learned in German, from the phrase book in a miniature airline dictionary, was: 'Have you found your sea legs yet?' At the time I had no idea what sea legs were or indeed why anyone might have lost them. These are typical examples of the kind of thing that communicative language teaching aspired to replace. The aim was to learn language that would actually enable you to communicate.

Typical of the kind of thing criticised by the communicative crusaders was the teacher who holds up a ruler and asks, 'What's this?' Or worse, asks, 'Is this an apple?' The argument was that you shouldn't ask stupid questions, and of course it is very tempting to reply, 'Bite it and see.' But the truth is that learning a language in a classroom is inevitably a very artificial experience. There is no point in pretending that the majority of exchanges that take place there are going to be realistic or, to use the jargon, 'authentic'. Many of the most effective games, dialogues and activities have a slightly crazy quality to them. But might that not be precisely why they are so enjoyable?

Take another example: songs. Everyone agrees that learning songs in French is both a popular and a useful activity. But what is communicative about singing a song together? Everyone is saying the same thing; there's

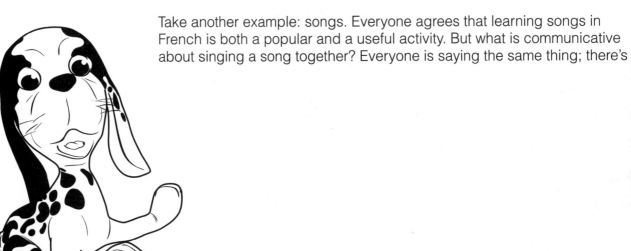

no personal expression or choice involved; they've been told what to say; and there's no exchange of meaning. But so what? To apply the 'communicative' test to singing a song is as pointless as testing a banana with a voltmeter before you eat it.

This is not to denigrate the great value of communicative activities – those in which learners are using language for a 'real purpose'. But 'real purpose' does not have to mean 'life-like activity'. They may be playing a game or carrying out a role play in which one partner has to find out certain information from the other. The information they are after may be fictitious or even fanciful. The important thing is that they really are trying to find out or to communicate something. There is, in other words, a reason for the talking they're doing.

Classroom language – the expressions you and your pupils use in the course of lessons – is the exception. If they can say in French that they need a pen, or that they don't understand, these are genuine, real-life communications. For this reason, and because it is an area of language that can naturally be reused day after day, it is important to treat it as a key topic in its own right. It is not just a means to the end of running the lesson in French – a way of oiling the wheels so they can learn other things. It is a valuable and important end in itself.

To sum up, as a general goal, it is clearly right to be equipping learners with the kind of language they will be able to use in real life: French should not feel like an academic exercise. But this does not mean that the activities you do to help them learn all have to be realistic or 'sensible'. The more they are using French with a real purpose (this includes in order to play a game) the better. The question to keep foremost in your mind is: does it work? Does it keep children interested and does it help them learn? If it does, do it.

What strategies are there for coping with problems of communication?

One thing that is certain when trying to communicate in a foreign language is that there will be many times when you don't understand and many more when you can't make yourself understood. Learning how to deal with this is an important skill in its own right. It is arguably as much a social skill as a language skill.

How to... overcome communication problems

Using gesture and expression – in effect, acting – is the most obvious strategy but mastering a few phrases designed specifically for stalling and buying time is also a good investment:

- *je veux dire ...* (I mean)
- *un moment* (just a minute)
- *oh là là* (oh dear)
- *désolé* (sorry)
- *c'est difficile* (it's hard)
- *je n'y arrive pas* (I can't do it)
- *euh* (the perennial French hesitation)

Encourage children to use these in class when they're having trouble expressing themselves, and praise them for using them well.

From early on, teach the key questions you'd need to ask a French speaker if you were having problems understanding:

- *Je ne comprends pas.* (I don't understand.)
- *Vous pouvez répéter, s'il vous plaît ?* (Can you say that again, please?)
- *Que veut dire 'sel' ?* (What does 'sel' mean?)

Whenever a child doesn't understand something, encourage them to use one of these expressions. After all, even communicating that you haven't understood or can't explain something is itself a successful communication.

Paraphrasing, or finding another way of saying something, is not only an important strategy but a fundamentally useful mental exercise. It's what you do when you're trying to write or speak well in your own language, and find yourself choosing between different ways of saying something. If you can't think of how to say 'slower, please' in French, you could say 'that's too fast'. If you've forgotten the word for 'when?' you can ask 'what day?' or 'what time?' It's worth discussing this kind of paraphrasing in English: ask children how else they can explain something, remembering the role that actions and facial expressions can play.

Last, but not least, comes a strategy that generally doesn't have a very good reputation in education, but which is important – indeed indispensable – in foreign language learning: guessing. Children will never cease to need it even if they go on to do a degree in languages. Help them to see that, using what they know about the context, they can make an informed guess at the meaning of an unfamiliar word or phrase. Be sure to teach the instruction *Devine !* or *Devinez !* (Guess!) in order to be able to encourage them in this essential skill.

How can I incorporate differentiation and personalisation?

What are the fundamental concepts behind these two terms? To let children develop at their own pace, work at their own level or pursue their own interests; to provide tasks which stimulate and challenge them but which enable them to enjoy success; to allow for the fact that different children have different strengths and weaknesses, and different learning styles… The list could go on. But how should they be accommodated into teaching French?

The first thing to say is that there is very little time for French in the school week. This in itself greatly reduces the opportunities for differentiation. Moreover, much of the best practice in primary languages involves whole-class activities and it would clearly be a shame to undermine this.

How can I address different learning styles?

Much is said and written about auditory, visual and kinaesthetic learning styles. The reality is that all children respond to not just one of these but to different combinations of all three. As a general rule, try to vary activity types to include examples of each in every lesson: the nature of the task will often determine which is most appropriate.

Another factor that complicates any desire to divide children into conventional ability groups is that their abilities can vary greatly from one skill to another. Academically able children are by no means necessarily the best or most confident communicators. Conversely, some children who are very confident orally will have difficulties with the written word while others who are shy at speaking may be very good at listening tasks. Given this and the limited time available, it is probably wise to restrict any group differentiation to the occasional reading and writing activity. Such considerations as whether answers are open or multiple choice, and whether a phrase needs writing or just identifying, can greatly affect the level of difficulty of a task.

How can I provide personalised learning?

Good interactive software offers every child the opportunity to work at their own pace, to exercise some personal choice about what they do, to try things a second or third time, and to make their mistakes – and learn from them – in private. Genuinely responsive software goes a long way to providing what is generally meant by personalisation.

It is, of course, important to personalise learning in the sense of enabling children to talk about themselves and their own lives. As far as encouraging them to express or pursue a personal interest within the subject concerned, this is not only made difficult by limitations of time but also by limitations of vocabulary (yours as well as the pupils'!). In the secondary curriculum, the classic problem area is jobs: 'Miss, how do you say "My Mum's a freelance catering consultant?"' But even in Key Stage 2, such areas as pets can throw up challenges to the teacher. A boy who has a pair of angel fish may settle for just saying that he has two fish, but what are you going to suggest for Tania who has

three ferrets and a terrapin? If that's what she's got, then that's what she'll want to be able to say. You will have to look it up or help her to look it up. Unfortunately, omniscience isn't an option.

Any project work which opens the doors to the pursuit of very personal interests is potentially fraught with such dangers. Unless you have a native speaker at hand, it is probably safest to avoid it.

Cross-curricular links

One of the advantages you as a primary teacher have over the secondary teacher is the ability to make links between different areas of the curriculum and thus to help children see that the knowledge and understanding they are building up is all part of a single web.

- The most obvious link to be made is that between literacy and French, in so far as their knowledge about one language is bound to illuminate their grasp of the other. They will inevitably see patterns common to both and will use their knowledge of one to identify the differences in the other. They will discover how they can use this knowledge (often unconsciously) to guess at meanings and predict how to say things.

- Use examples from French life and culture in areas such as geography and history, and when dealing with topics like food, sport or holidays. Once children are learning the language, they will naturally develop a greater curiosity about the places where it is spoken. Many things French are now familiar to British children, from French footballers to French bread. Make the most of what they already know and use this as a springboard for further exploration.

- Doing a simple activity in French rather than English can be an effective way of making it feel fresh. Try mental maths or Brain Gym® in French, or even, if you sometimes use a countdown technique to obtain silence, why not do that in French?

Intercultural understanding

While it is important to encourage a curiosity about other cultures, it is easy to forget that, out of context, the way people do things in other countries isn't necessarily fascinating to a child. What French cheese looks (or smells) like, what a French policeman wears, what time shops open, why houses have shutters, how the French celebrate New Year – all these are matters that may or may not interest them.

Arguably the term 'understanding' is misplaced here. What we might hope children will develop is more of a 'feel' for and a curiosity about the culture and the country than a real 'understanding' of it. Indeed, such questions as how the French can, on occasion, express genuine social solidarity and yet struggle with the principle of queuing, remain perennially difficult to answer.

Generally speaking, it is when 'cultural information' is embedded in something which has captured children's imagination that it becomes of interest to them. A story, song or poem that refers to a tradition like *carnaval* or *poisson d'avril* is more likely to spark children's curiosity than a factual presentation. Let's be honest: do you really care what the Belgians do at Easter? Like us, children need a reason to be interested in things.

One of the benefits of learning a foreign language is that it breaks down the preconception that 'our way of doing things is normal; other people's way is silly'. Enshrined in the 'Intercultural understanding' strand of the

KS2 Framework, this applies to language as much as it does to national habits and customs. If children can come to realise how arbitrary or strange some of the things about their own language and culture are, the more open they will become to another and the less hasty to judge.

The insanity of English spelling is easy enough to illustrate. Among the many examples of English usage which must strike foreigners as particularly odd is that you can 'cut a tree down' and then 'cut it up'. Turning back to French after acknowledging such things as this can do a great deal to open children's minds.

Assessment

A great deal is written about so-called formative and summative assessment, though the distinction is far from clear. When does ordinary classroom interaction become formative assessment – when you make a note of a child's response? When you record grades? What makes a test summative – telling children a week in advance that it will take place next? Writing the results in a mark book? Doing it at the end of a unit or a term? Or simply calling it 'a test'?

Assessment, of course, is important for both teacher and learners. As a teacher you need to know whether children are learning successfully and children need to see that they are making progress, but they cannot measure this progress without help. The key questions are therefore:

- What types of assessment is it best to do?
- How often should you assess?
- How should you record the results?

First of all, ensure that assessment reflects proportionately the skills children are practising in class: if they are mainly listening and speaking, don't try to measure their progress with a reading or writing test. Speaking is difficult to assess because it can only be done individually and is therefore time consuming. For this reason, try to record a comment or grade when children are doing paired-speaking work in class. It is important to make children aware that these observations can contribute to the overall assessment.

End-of-term tests or end-of-topic tests, if effective, should give children a sense of their own achievement. The legitimate concern many teachers have about any whole-class test is that the results risk being discouraging for weaker children who are nonetheless making a real effort. Giving greater credit for success at communication and less to accuracy (see page 26) is one way of counterbalancing this concern. But children who aspire to accuracy need to feel that their efforts are valued too. There is no reason why the value of both cannot be acknowledged and openly discussed.

Various schemes and systems exist to help teacher and children chart their progress. Some regions and authorities have devised their own assessment tools. At a national level, *The Languages Ladder* is a government-approved scheme and is in line with the wider *European Language Portfolio*. It identifies children's achievement through a series of 'can do' statements for each skill at each grade. Asset Languages, administered by OCR, offers materials, training and accreditation for both assessment by the teacher, leading to Grade Awards, and for external assessment. It is designed to complement, not to replace, existing schemes of work and qualifications. More information can be found at: www.assetlanguages.org.uk

Self-assessment

Self-assessment is every bit as important as teacher assessment. Keeping a record of what children have learned creates a real sense of progress. The end of a topic is the natural point to do this. It can be done in a series of 'I can' statements, measuring their attainment of a range of objectives in terms like 'yes', 'partly' and 'not yet'. It is worth introducing a system whereby parents get to see these self-evaluation sheets too.

A degree of self-assessment is implied, of course, in the value placed by the KS2 Framework on learning strategies. In thinking about and discussing which techniques have proved most effective in their learning, children are necessarily judging their own progress and achievement. They are in effect saying, 'I learned this because…' or 'I didn't learn this because…' Such awareness helps to make the idea of measuring progress less threatening.

Good interactive software can make a major contribution to self assessment. It enables children to work at their own speed, to try things again and improve on their performance – and at the same time it can keep a constantly updated record of their achievement. Given the opportunity, children will continue to work on enjoyable software at home and this, of course, can go a long way to addressing the problem of the inadequate time allocation for languages in the school timetable.

Summary

There is not only one correct way of teaching French but there are a number of dos and don'ts that can help you. Some of them apply, of course, to any subject.

Do...

- Conduct as much of the lesson as you can in French.

Vary the tasks and keep them short.

- Praise children (in French!) for their achievements.
- Use a combination of visual, auditory and kinaesthetic activities to ensure that children who favour different learning styles are catered for.
- Give them time to hear and get used to new vocabulary before expecting them to 'produce' it.
- Ensure that children have a chance to use language themselves and not just to hear or read it.
- Regularly return to topics and language they have learned before, to keep it fresh in their minds and to give them a sense of their progress.
- Make children feel they are allowed to make mistakes.
- Provide them with opportunities to practise and consolidate their learning in their own time using interactive software. The old adage 'practice makes perfect' is especially true for language learning.

Don't...

- Focus on children's mistakes.
- Make them afraid to have a go.
- Expect children to understand every word.
- Expect them to remember everything.
- Inflict death by assessment.

How good does my French have to be?

Combating feeling rusty

If your French dates back to school days and has not been used much since beginning to teach, it may feel like getting an old bike out of the garage and wondering about riding it. *Does it matter that it's rusty? Is it too old-fashioned? Can I figure out how the gears work? Do they work? Will I remember how to ride it?*

It would be dishonest to pretend that a good level of competence in the language would not be an advantage. The practical question is: is a lower level of competence going to be a problem? The true answer to *this* question is that it depends how you set about teaching it.

In the same way that you would ensure or prepare your own knowledge before launching into a topic about map-reading or the Vikings, it is obviously important to identify the vocabulary, grammar and cultural background associated with any given topic in French. This should be quite manageable and, if you are dealing with beginners, you should quite easily be able to stay ahead of the game.

Worrying about your accent

Make it clear to your pupils that the authentic French speakers in the recordings you use are the model for them to follow. Unless you are bilingual, it will be obvious to them as soon as they hear these that your own accent and mastery of the language are not perfect. There is no point in trying to pretend it is but nor is there any reason to apologise for it.

Making mistakes

There will be moments when you are aware of making a mistake or at least suspect you have made one. If no one questions it, don't worry. If somebody does, how frankly you can acknowledge it will depend on your relationship with the class. In either case, it is not the end of the world. A word of reassurance: French people make mistakes in their language too. My children went to school in France and, in writing, lots of their friends constantly forgot the silent letters at the ends of words, mixed up *c'est* and *ses*, *à* and *a*, *on* and *ont*, and so on. They lost marks in exams but daily life never penalised them too much.

Conducting lessons in French

What you will probably find most demanding is the knowledge required to use French to actually conduct the lesson (see page 20 for why this is desirable). Even people whose French is good find that the language needed in the classroom is very specific and different from anything they will have used elsewhere. The 'Classroom language' section on the accompanying CD-ROM directly addresses this problem and provides interactive practice to help you to build up the repertoire you will need. All the expressions included there are also listed below (see pages 44–47).

Most teachers find that teaching the language motivates them to want to improve their own skill in any case. This may be by attending a continuing professional development course, by spending time in France or by pursuing some form of self study.

Worrying about grammar

For those whose confidence about basic grammar is shaky, it may help to remember that the vast majority of French grammar you need to be aware of falls into two categories:

Agreement relating to gender or number

A host of words – from determinants (the, a) to adjectives and possessive adjectives (good, all, my, your) – change their spelling and sometimes their pronunciation depending on whether they refer to a masculine or a feminine, a singular or a plural word. These changes tend to follow broad patterns, though of course there are many annoying exceptions. Errors in this area rarely lead to a failure of communication.

Verbs

Verbs change their endings and sometimes their whole spellings depending on *person* (I, you, he/she, we, you (pl.), they) and on *tense* (past, present, future). For the needs of the primary curriculum, your use of verbs will be largely restricted to the present tense. But you will need to become confident in all six 'persons' of the standard verb. The formation of negatives and of questions are areas you will need to be competent in as well.

If this alarms you, remember that one of the key skills of language learning is finding ways of saying what you want with the limited means at your disposal. Sometimes this even extends to deciding *not* to say what you'd like to, because you don't know how to. Sometimes gestures and expressions may come to the rescue. If children adopt the same strategy, consider it a good lesson learned.

Classroom language

It is not suggested that you need to know all the expressions listed below in order to begin teaching – in any case, you can only expect pupils to pick up one or two at a time. However, the more you can build up your own knowledge of them, the more at ease you will become conducting your lessons in French. You can listen to the pronunciation of all these phrases on the accompanying CD-ROM.

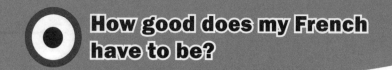

Useful phrases

Pas de problème.	No problem.
Allez …	Right then… /Come on.
Je m'excuse.	Sorry.
Désolé(e).	Sorry.
C'est la récré.	It's playtime.
C'est l'heure de manger.	It's time for lunch.
Continue.	Carry on. (sing.)
Continuez.	Carry on. (pl.)
Réfléchis.	Think (about it). (sing.)
Réfléchissez.	Think(about it). (pl.)

Greetings and farewells

Bonjour, tout le monde.	Hello, everybody.
Bonjour, les enfants !	Hello, children!
Bienvenue !	Welcome!
Ça va ?	Are you all right?/How are you?
Sam est absent ?	Is Sam away?
Où est Sam ?	Where's Sam?
Au revoir !	Goodbye!
Bonne journée !	Have a nice day!
A lundi.	See you on Monday.

Asking questions I

Qui sait ?	Who knows?
Qui veut répondre ?	Who wants to answer?
Qui veut commencer ?	Who wants to start?
Qui a fini ?	Who has finished?
Tu as fini ?	Have you finished? (sing.)
Vous avez fini ?	Have you finished? (pl.)
Vous êtes prêts ?	Are you ready? (pl.)
Tu comprends ?	Do you understand? (sing.)
Vous comprenez ?	Do you understand? (pl.)

Asking questions II

Qui comprend ?	Who understands?
Qu'est-ce qu'il y a ?	What's the matter?
Comment ?	Pardon?
Comment dit-on 'moi' en anglais ?	How do you say 'moi' in English?
Comment dit-on 'who?' en français ?	How do you say 'who' in French?
Comment ça s'écrit ?	How do you spell that?
Ça s'écrit o-u-i.	It's spelt o-u-i.
Que veut dire 'combien' ?	What does 'combien'mean?

Moving around the classroom I

Assieds-toi.	Sit down. (sing.)
Asseyez-vous.	Sit down. (pl.)
Lève-toi.	Stand up. (sing.)
Levez-vous.	Stand up. (pl.)

Retourne-toi.	Turn round. (sing.)
Retournez-vous.	Turn round. (pl.)
Viens devant.	Come to the front. (sing.)
Venez devant.	Come to the front. (pl.)
Mettez-vous deux par deux.	Get into pairs.
Mettez-vous par quatre.	Get into groups of four.

Moving around the classroom II

On va jouer à un jeu.	We're going to play a game.
On va continuer.	We're going to carry on.
Vas-y.	Go on. (sing.)
Allez-y.	Go on. (pl.)
Reste là.	Stay there. (sing.)
Restez là.	Stay there. (pl.)
Retourne à ta place.	Go back to your place. (sing.)
Retournez à vos places.	Go back to your places. (pl.)
Attends.	Wait. (sing.)
Attendez.	Wait. (pl.)

Moving around the classroom III

Formez un cercle.	Get into a circle.
Mettez-vous en ligne.	Get into a line.
Levez la main.	Put up your hands.
Levez le doigt.	Put up your hands.
Baissez les mains.	Hands down.
Sortez vos affaires.	Get your things out.
Rangez vos affaires.	Put your things away.

Speaking and listening I

Parle plus fort.	Speak louder. (sing.)
Parlez plus fort.	Speak louder. (pl.)
Répète.	Say it again. (sing.)
Répétez.	Say it again. (pl.)
Tous ensemble.	All together.
Tout le monde.	Everybody.
Ecoutez la cassette.	Listen to the cassette.
Ecoutez le CD.	Listen to the CD.
Ecoutez la conversation.	Listen to the conversation.
Ecoutez-moi.	Listen to me.
Ecoutez bien.	Listen carefully.

Speaking and listening II

Fais attention.	Pay attention. (sing.)
Faites attention.	Pay attention. (pl.)
C'est bon ?	Is that right?
Oui, c'est bon.	Yes, that's right.
Non, ce n'est pas bon.	No, it's not right.
Essaie encore.	Try again. (sing.)
Essayez encore.	Try again. (pl.)
Encore une fois.	Again.

How good does my French have to be?

Looking

Regardez le tableau.	Look at the board.
Regardez la page dix.	Look at page ten.
Regardez-moi.	Look at me.
Regardez la feuille.	Look at the sheet.
Regardez les mots.	Look at the words.
Regardez les images.	Look at the pictures.

Reading and writing

Lisez le texte.	Read the text. (pl.)
Lis-le à voix haute.	Read it out loud. (sing.)
Prenez vos stylos.	Take your pens.
Prenez vos crayons.	Take your pencils.
Posez vos stylos.	Put your pens down.
Posez vos crayons.	Put your pencils down.
Tu n'as pas de stylo ?	Haven't you got a pen?
On va le corriger.	We're going to mark. it
Ecrivez vos prénoms.	Write your first name. (pl.)
Ecris ton prénom.	Write your first name. (sing.)
L'alphabet: a, b, c …	The alphabet: a, b, c…

Praise

C'est bien.	Good.
Super.	Great.
Excellent !	Excellent!
Génial !	Great!
Fantastique !	Fantastic!
C'est parfait !	That's perfect!
C'est ça.	That's it.
C'est bon.	That's right.
Pas mal.	Not bad.
Pas tout à fait.	Not quite.

Censure

Oh là là !	Dear oh dear!
Arrête !	Stop it! (sing.)
Arrêtez !	Stop it! (pl.)
Calme-toi !	Settle down! (sing.)
Calmez-vous !	Settle down! (pl.)
Silence !	Silence!
Ça suffit !	That's enough!/That'll do!

Special occasions

A tes souhaits !	Bless you!
Bon anniversaire !	Happy birthday!
Félicitations !	Congratulations!

Pupil language

Basic communications

Monsieur.	Sir.
Madame.	Miss.
Présent.	Here. (m)
Présente.	Here. (f)
Absent.	Absent. (m)
Absente.	Absent. (f)
Il est malade.	He's ill.
Elle est malade.	She's ill.
Comment ?	Pardon?
J'ai fini.	I've finished.
Excusez-moi.	I'm sorry.
Merci.	Thank you.

Asking for help

Qu'est-ce que ça veut dire ?	What does that mean?
Est-ce que je peux aller aux toilettes ?	May I go to the toilet?
Pouvez-vous m'aider, sil vous plaît ?	Can you help me, please?
Pouvez-vous répéter, sil vous plaît ?	Can you repeat that, please?
Vous pouvez répéter, s'il vous plaît ?	Can you say that again, please?

When having difficulties I

Je veux dire …	I mean…
Un moment.	Just a minute.
Oh là là.	Oh dear.
C'est difficile.	It's hard.
Je n'y arrive pas.	I can't do it.
Je ne comprends pas.	I don't understand.

When having difficulties II

Je ne sais pas.	I don't know.
Je suis coincé(e).	I'm stuck.
Je n'ai pas de stylo.	I haven't got a pen.
Je n'ai pas de crayon.	I haven't got a pencil.
J'ai oublié ma trousse.	I've forgotten my pencil case.
Je n'ai pas fait mes devoirs.	I haven't done my homework.

Sample units and lesson plans

How to use these lessons

This chapter provides detailed lesson plans for three units:

- Numbers
- Colours
- Parts of the body

As well as explaining the practicalities of 'what to do', importantly, each section contains advice about methodology. For example, next to the suggestions as to how to use a particular song, a special section considers the use of songs in general. By following this advice, activities can easily be adapted to fit other topics and themes.

Language acquisition is inevitably cumulative: it makes sense to build on what you've learned before and to avoid things you haven't. If you follow these lesson plans, it is therefore best to keep to the order proposed. The second unit, 'Colours', assumes knowledge of numbers and the third unit, 'Parts of the body', assumes knowledge of both numbers and colours. This recycling of previous learning should be at the heart of any effective scheme of work for a language.

If you are already using a scheme of work, these plans and materials can be used to complement it. But if you are launching into the teaching of French for the first time, they can be relied on to provide all you need to teach these three units. They assume only that you will have taught the basics of saying your name, saying hello and goodbye, plus a few basic classroom commands and comments. These last can be practised using the 'Classroom language' section of the CD-ROM.

The proposed sequence of activities is divided into lesson plans by way of example. Of course, offering precise lesson plans is asking for trouble since not only will different teachers have different amounts of time available but also no two classes will get through the same things in any given time. What's more, many teachers find the 'little and often' approach more effective than once- or even twice-weekly lessons. Do not feel constrained, therefore, if you choose to teach French in more, shorter sessions or if your timetable prevents you from following the lesson plans closely. Feel free to select or modify the activities to suit your circumstances and preferences. Equally, you have the choice of doing all three units one after the other or of developing each further before moving on.

Resources

All these activities are supported by a variety of resources which are provided on the accompanying CD-ROM as well as photocopiable resources on pages 78–91. There are:

- 14 photocopiable worksheets (photocopy from pages 78–91 or print from the CD-ROM);
- 12 flashcards (print from the CD-ROM);
- 7 audio tracks (on the CD-ROM);
- 13 interactive games and activities (on the CD-ROM).

Photocopiable pages

Title	Page number	Unit
Loto	78	Numbers
Les nombres	79	Numbers
Dix euros (chanson)	80	Numbers
Découvre le numéro !	81	Numbers
Calculs	82	Numbers
Mots croisés	83	Numbers
Jeu	84	Numbers
Jeu des couleurs	85	Colours
Mots croisés	86	Colours
Colorie l'image.	87	Colours
Le corps	88	Parts of the body
Rap (chanson)	89	Parts of the body
Un robot et un monstre	90	Parts of the body
Qu'est-ce qui manque ?	91	Parts of the body

Activities on CD-ROM

The CD-ROM activities work best if used on an interactive whiteboard although children will also benefit from doing the activities individually.

Unit 1 lesson 1

Objective

To learn, orally, the numbers from 1 to 10.

Materials needed

● Beanbag or soft ball;
● 10 objects of the same kind, such as books or bottles.

Starter

● Use objects or your fingers to introduce the numbers 1 to 3. Place the objects on the desk, saying the numbers as you do so: *un, deux, trois.*

● Do this again, asking the class to repeat it after you: *Répétez : un, deux, trois.*

● Next, hold up different numbers of objects or fingers and elicit the correct French word. Always praise children in French: *Bien ! / Super ! / Oui !*

● Continue with numbers 4 to 6, asking the class to repeat after you: *quatre, cinq, six.*

● Then count from 1 to 6, leading the counting the first time and then letting the children take the lead.

● Again, hold up different numbers of objects or fingers to elicit the French.

● Then move on to numbers 7, 8, 9 and 10, using the same procedure: *sept, huit, neuf, dix.*

● Finally, count together all the way from 1 to 10.

● Explain that you want a different child to give each number as you count up to 10. Ask them to put up their hands to volunteer the next number. Select a child to begin, then another, and so on. When you get to ten, start again.

● Children who think they can recite the whole ten alone may already like to try it but don't force anybody into it.

● Encourage them to pronounce the words as accurately as possible. The numbers provide excellent examples of some of the key French sounds: the nasal *un, cinq*; the 'r' in *trois* and *quatre*; the pout of the lips required for *deux, trois, huit* and *neuf*. Repeating them for pronunciation purposes also means the children hear them plenty of times and so have a better chance of remembering them.

Methodology: using different activity types

● When introducing any new language it is important to use a number of different ways of practising and reinforcing it. This is not only for the sake of variety, but because every child will find one approach more effective than another.

● One popular technique is to vary the volume and expression of your voice when modelling new vocabulary: whispering the word, shouting it, saying it in a commanding, questioning, relieved, surprised, disappointed, frightened, sleepy or amused tone. The children then imitate this tone as well as the sound of the word itself. While very effective, this, like any technique, is best used sparingly and not every single time you teach new words.

CD-ROM

'Un, deux, trois … ' (Audio track 1)

Play the recording so the children can hear the numbers pronounced by a native speaker.

> ## Transcript
> *Un, deux, trois, quatre, cinq, six, sept, huit, neuf, dix.*

CD-ROM 💿

● Audio track 1: 'Un, deux, trois … ';
● Interactive activity 1: 'Clique écoute et répète'.

'Clique, écoute et répète' (Interactive activity 1) 💿

● Ask the children to select a number to hear its name.

● Then name a number and ask for a volunteer to come to the interactive whiteboard and identify it. By touching it, the audio will confirm their choice.

Practice games

● Play a circle game with a ball or beanbag. Say *un* as you throw it to the first child, who then says *deux* as they throw it to the second, and so on up to *dix*.

● Play *'Ouaf ! '* (the sound of a dog barking, pronounced 'Wuff'). In circles of six or seven, children take turns to count from one to ten. Each time they reach a specified 'forbidden number' or any number divisible by five (then four, then three), they have to say *ouaf* instead. So it goes, for example, *un, deux, trois, quatre, ouaf ! six, sept, huit, neuf, ouaf !* If a child says a 'forbidden number', they are out and the counting begins again. Change the forbidden number after a certain time.

Unit 1 lesson 2

Objectives

● To revise the numbers from 1 to 10 orally.
● To learn the written forms of the numbers from 1 to 10.

Materials needed

● 'Loto' photocopiable 1 (page 78);
● 'Les nombres' photocopiable 2 (page 79).

Starter

● Ask the children to work in pairs, and take it in turns to count to 10, as if counting the strokes in a table tennis rally. They should then do the action of hitting the ball as they say the numbers.

● Go round the classroom giving every child a number between one and ten. Then call out a number. Everyone who has that number has to stand up. After a while a child can be given the job of calling out the numbers.

'Ecoute et clique' (Interactive activity 2)

● This is a good activity for building children's confidence. Ask one child at a time to try and burst the correct bubble as they hear the number.

● Alternatively, stand one child on each side of the board and challenge them to be the first to burst it. This could be played as a team game, with points awarded.

● As well as playing as a whole class on the interactive whiteboard, the children will enjoy and benefit from playing this game on their own: they will learn more from doing it themselves than from watching others do it.

'Loto' (Photocopiable page 78)

This sheet provides six empty grids for playing bingo, known as *Loto* in French. By playing this game every child will be involved in number recognition.

● Cut up the sheets and distribute a grid to each child. Ask them to write the number 1 in any square, then the number 2, and so on up to 10, until the grid is full. (The children should black out the two remaining squares.) Demonstrate by filling in a grid on the board.

● Tell them that you are going to call out numbers and that they must put a line through each number you call. The first person to cross out all the numbers in one horizontal line – and call out *Loto* ! – is the winner.

● You may want to offer a small prize to the winner. The game can then be played again using a new grid.

'Un, deux, trois … ' (Audio track 1); 'Les nombres' (Photocopiable page 79)

● Give one sheet to each child. They can now look at the written forms of the numbers as they listen again to their pronunciation by a native speaker.

● Point out the silent last letters of *deux* and *trois*. They can then colour in the numbers on the sheet.

Intercultural understanding: writing the numbers

All French children learn to write the number one in two strokes and the number seven with a crossbar (though they are like our own when printed).

You may like to do this yourself when writing them on the board, so the children get used to their appearance. They will meet the French 7 in 'Découvre le numéro' on page 81.

If asked why the 7 has a crossbar, explain that it is to distinguish it from the 1 which, with its top stroke, might otherwise easily be mistaken for it.

17

CD-ROM

● Audio track 1: 'Un, deux, trois … ';
● Interactive activity 2: 'Ecoute et clique'.

Practice game

● If the children are familiar with the concept of odd and even numbers (in French, *impair* and *pair*), play the following game. Draw on the board and demonstrate an 'arms above you' position and explain they should do this when they hear an odd number (*un nombre impair*). Draw and demonstrate the 'arms out sideways' position they should adopt when they hear an even number (*un nombre pair*). Practise this with several examples.

● Then call out a series of numbers to which the children have to respond with the appropriate gesture.

● You can play this as an elimination game if you wish.

Methodology: introducing the written form

The value of children seeing the written form of words they are learning is primarily as a support for the spoken word. Most children will find that seeing the word written will help them to fix it in their minds. It is not, therefore, a matter of moving from the spoken to the written word as some kind of progression in itself. Other, more demanding activities of a purely oral nature will still have their place even after children have learned to recognise the written forms.

Unit 1 lesson 3

Objectives

- To gain confidence with the written forms of numbers from 1 to 10.
- To learn a counting song in French.

Materials needed

- 'Dix euros' photocopiable 3 (page 80);
- 'Découvre le numéro !' photocopiable 4 (page 81).

Starter

- Write the numbers from 1 to 10 on the board.
- Divide the class into teams and ask one representative of each team to come to the board.
- When you call out a number, the first child to point to it, cross it out or rub it out wins a point for their team.

'Dix, neuf, huit … ' (Audio track 2)

- Write the numbers on the board in reverse order, as for a rocket launch. You could encourage the children to supply the name of the next number as you go.
- Ask the children what they think *zéro* and *feu !* (literally fire!) mean. The word *zéro* may well be the first one they have met which includes a French accent. It is worth pointing out that this mark is an essential part of the spelling of the word and that it tells you how to pronounce the letter. Give them the chance of writing it themselves.
- Play the recording of the countdown and ask them to follow the numbers with their finger.
- Now they can join in with the recording and chant the countdown in unison. Follow up by getting them to chant it without the recording.
- Finally, remove the written form of the numbers and write up the digits 10 to 0 instead. They can then chant the countdown together without the support of the written words.

> ### Transcript
> *Dix ! Neuf ! Huit ! Sept ! Six ! Cinq ! Quatre ! Trois ! Deux ! Un ! Zéro ! Feu !*

'Dix euros' (Audio track 3); 'Dix euros' (Interactive activity 3); 'Dix euros' (Photocopiable page 80)

- The best way to introduce a song is to let the children hear it – or at least part of it. The song 'Dix euros' is presented in a singalong form on the CD-ROM and the text is also provided on photocopiable page 80. It is also recorded in the audio section. You can decide in which form you prefer to present it but in any case practise the pronunciation before showing them the written word. You will need to explain the meaning of the new language before asking the children to join in. (The word *combien* will be used actively in the next lesson.)

- Two obviously French phenomena are introduced in the song: the currency, *euros*, and the *pain au chocolat*. By far the best way to illustrate these, if possible, is to bring in an actual *pain au chocolat* and a few euro coins.

- Don't be put off by the fact that one or two expressions in the song may appear more complex: to a child they are just expressions, not grammar. They will simply learn them through repetition. In this song only one word – the number – changes in each verse (except for the last verse in which the final line changes too).

- Tell the children to repeat each line after you several times, then read through the whole of the first verse together. You can then play the music again and encourage the class to sing along.

- Point out (if the children themselves do not) the cedilla under the c in *ça* and explain that it softens the c to an s sound.

CD-ROM

- Audio track 2: 'Dix, neuf, huit … ';
- Audio track 3: 'Dix euros';
- Interactive activity 3: 'Dix euros'.

Translation (also see 'Dix euros' on page 80 for a full transcript)

Verse 1

Dix euros,	Ten euros,
Ça ne va pas loin.	That doesn't go far.
Prends un pain au chocolat.	Get a *pain au chocolat*.
Il te reste combien ?	How much have you got left?

Verse 10

Un euro,	One euro,
Ça ne va pas loin.	That doesn't go far.
Prends un pain au chocolat.	Get a *pain au chocolat*.
Il ne te reste rien !	You've got nothing left!

'Découvre le numéro ! ' (Photocopiable page 81)

- In this puzzle, the children have to join up the numbered dots according to the list to reveal the hidden number. They then write the name of the number (as a word, in French) on the dotted line.

- You may want to demonstrate the first line (drawing a vertical from 10 to 7) as an example.

Answers

1: *un* 3: *trois*
2: *sept* 4: *neuf*

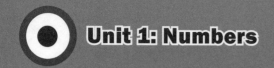

Unit 1 lesson 4

Starter

- Ask the children to count down from 10 to 0 in pairs, taking turns to say the numbers:

> Child A: *Dix*
> Child B: *Neuf*
> Child A: *Huit*
> Child B: *Sept ...*
> etc.

- When the children get to zero, they could start counting up again: *trois, deux, un, zéro, un, deux* and so on.
- Teach numbers 11 (*onze*) and 12 (*douze*), writing the figures on the board. You may like to ask the children if they can see any connection with other numbers: *un → onze ; deux → douze.*
- Do some simple mental maths with the class.
- Teach the word *plus* using the mathematical sign +.
- Then ask *Un plus un ? Deux plus deux ?* and so on. Encourage the children to be the first to put their hand up. Make sure the totals don't go beyond twelve!
- To make it more exciting, pause before you say the second number, for example, *Quatre plus ... six ?*

'Dix euros' (Audio track 3)

- Sing the song again.
- Write the numbers 10 to 1 on the board and prompt each verse by pointing to the appropriate number.
- Ask the children to hold up the appropriate number of fingers as they sing each verse and do a gesture to represent taking the *pain au chocolat* on the third line.

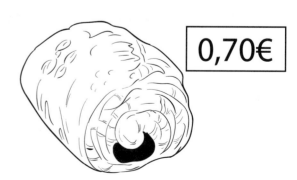

0,70€

'Calculs' (Photocopiable page 82)

CD-ROM

Audio track 3:
'Dix euros'.

- This page includes ten additions and subtractions using the written form of the numbers. You can either work through these together or leave the children to do them on their own – or a combination of these. In any case, it is a good idea to do the first one together as an example.

Answers

1: *trois*

2: *onze*

3: *neuf*

4: *deux*

5: *dix*

6: *onze*

7: *douze*

8: *douze*

9: *sept*

10: *zéro*

'Mots croisés (1)' (Photocopiable page 83)

- The crossword contains the numbers from 1 to 12. There are no clues: the children simply have to work out how all the numbers will fit in to the grid.

- The written numbers appear at the bottom of the sheet for support. To make the task more demanding, these could be cut off.

- You may want to help them to fill in a first word. Rather than simply supply it, why not ask: *Where will the number one fit in?* There's only one place for a two-letter word. Once this is in place, ask (if necessary): *Which word has 'u' as its second letter?*

Answers

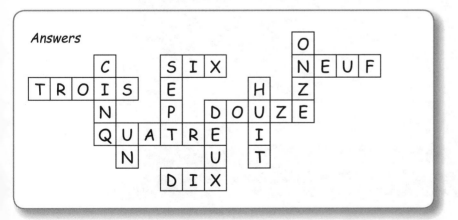

Unit 1 lesson 5

Objectives

- To learn the expression *combien de*.
- To be able to play a board game, counting in French.

Materials needed

- 'Jeu' photocopiable 7 (page 84);
- Two dice for each pair or group;
- One counter, coin or marker for each child.

Starter

- Tell the children that you are going to say a number. The person you point to must then say the one that follows. Give two or three examples, allowing volunteers to answer:

> Teacher: *Dix*
> Child A: *Onze*
> Teacher: *Six*
> Child B: *Sept ...*
> etc.

This game also works for letters of the alphabet, days of the week and months.

- Begin by asking who can remember the meaning of the word *combien*. (They have sung it in every verse of 'Dix euros'.)
- Consolidate this by holding up different numbers of fingers and asking: *Combien ?*

'Ecoute et clique sur le nombre'
(Interactive activity 4)

- Play 'Ecoute et clique sur le nombre' on the interactive whiteboard. The children have to say how many there are of the items shown but do not need to be able to name the items. Ask them: *Combien ?*
- In some cases, you may like to introduce the noun too, for example: *Combien de maisons ?* (How many houses?)

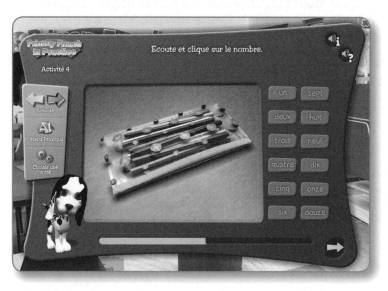

'Jeu' (Photocopiable page 84)

- The children can play this version of *Snakes and Ladders* in pairs or groups of three or four. Give each pair or group a sheet and a pair of dice. Tell them that when they roll the dice they must say the number in French, then count aloud as they move along the squares.

- You may wish to impose the following rule: if a number is said in English, the player has to go backwards by that number of squares.

- The children may subsequently like to colour in the board.

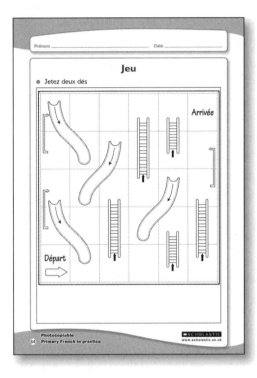

CD-ROM

- Interactive activity 4: 'Ecoute et clique sur le nombre';
- Audio track 3: 'Dix euros'.

'Dix euros'
(Audio track 3)

- End the sequence of lessons for this unit by singing the song 'Dix euros' together. The children should now be feeling confident enough with the words to give a really rousing rendering of it!

Recycling through song

It is, of course, essential to find ways of keeping all new language alive in children's minds by recycling it. Ideally, this means integrating it into a new context, though short, independent starter activities can be effective too. Compared to many topics, numbers are easy to reintroduce in other contexts, but for any topic, songs are an ideal way of revising over prior learning. Not only are children usually happy to sing again a song they have learned – it is even questionable what the point of learning it was if you're not going to sing it again! And the more familiar it becomes, the less they have to think about it and the more they'll enjoy it!

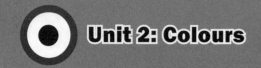

Unit 2 lesson 1

Objective

To learn, orally, six colours in French.

Materials needed

Flashcards 1–6, 12 (print from the CD-ROM).

Starter

- Begin by presenting the colours red, white and blue. Hold up the flashcards (1–3) and ask the children to repeat the colours as you say them: *rouge* (red), *blanc* (white), *bleu* (blue).

- When they are confident with pronouncing the words, show one at a time in random order and ask the children *C'est bleu ou blanc ?* (Is it blue or white?), *C'est rouge ou bleu ?* (Is it red or blue?) and so on.

- Show a colour and ask them to name it. Speed this up so they have to think really quickly.

- Before moving on, ask the children in English if they know what these three colours have to do with France. Show flashcard 12 of the French flag to confirm or provide the answer.

- Now introduce the next three colours using flashcards 4–6, green, yellow and black: *vert* (green), *jaune* (yellow), *noir* (black), asking the class to repeat them. Follow the same procedure as above.

- Mix in the first three colours again and play a yes/no game: explain that you are going to show a flashcard and say the name of a colour. If the name matches the colour, the children call out *Oui*; if it doesn't they call *Non*. If necessary, clarify the meaning of *Oui* and *Non* by nodding and shaking your head.

- Now show one colour at a time and ask the children to name it: *C'est quelle couleur ?* (What colour is it?)

Methodology: constructing a sequence that moves from receptive to productive tasks

- The stages suggested above for teaching the colours illustrate the progression from receptive activities (those in which the children just have to respond to the French) to productive activities (in which they actually have to come up with it themselves). It is advisable to follow this principle when introducing new vocabulary. It is only common sense, after all, to allow them to absorb and get used to the new words before putting them on the spot (see page 28).

- How soon children are willing to be 'exposed' by having to try and summon up a word themselves will depend as much on your relationship with the class as on their individual personalities. For this reason, it is important to create an environment in which they feel it is perfectly all right to have a go and get it wrong.

- Some people advocate a regular pattern of activity types when teaching new vocabulary. In my view there is a danger of this becoming boring – for the teacher as well as the pupils. Providing you observe the receptive-to-productive rule, there is no reason why you shouldn't vary the actual activities. Besides, some vocabulary will require more practice than others.

Practice games

- To recycle French numbers, draw the following on the whiteboard or on a large sheet of paper:

  A black number 1

  A red number 2

  A blue number 3

  A green number 4

  A yellow number 5

CD-ROM

Flashcards 1–6, 12.

Explain that you are going to say a sum using colours instead of numbers and that the children have to give the answer in French. Give the example: *noir plus rouge*. If necessary, talk the children through it, writing up:

Noir = 1

Rouge = 2

Noir + rouge   = 1 + 2 = trois

Now ask:

Noir plus bleu (answer: *quatre*)

Jaune plus rouge (answer: *sept*)

Vert plus bleu (answer: *sept*)

Noir plus jaune (answer: *six*)

Vert plus jaune (answer: *neuf*)

Bleu plus jaune (answer: *huit*)

Rouge plus bleu (answer: *cinq*)

Next, introduce *moins* (minus):

Vert moins noir (answer: *trois*)

Vert moins rouge (answer: *deux*)

Rouge moins noir (answer: *un*)

Bleu moins noir (answer: *deux*)

This can be conducted as a team game, in small groups.

- Follow this up by telling the children, in pairs or groups, to set each other mental maths questions using the same code. Games like this have the advantage of making them really think. Although the vocabulary involved is simple, the mental activity can be a genuine challenge.

Unit 2 lesson 2

Objectives

● To learn the written form of the first six colours.
● To learn the oral form of five new colours.

Materials needed

Flashcards 1–11 (print from the CD-ROM).

Starter

● Stand or stick up flashcards 1–6 in a row at the front of the class. Ask a volunteer and say: *Où est le … vert ?* (Where is the… green?) The child has to point to the right card. Continue using all six colours.

● Next, introduce the spelling of these six colours, writing them on the board as you say them and asking the children to copy them down. Ask the children what they notice about the last letter in the words *vert* and *blanc* (they are silent). Seeing the written forms will help many children to remember the words before you introduce more colours orally.

● Now introduce the next three colours: *rose* (pink), *orange* (orange) and *gris* (grey) in the same way as before (see below). Two are very close to the English. Ask the children where they think the French word for pink (*rose*) comes from.

● Ask the children to listen and repeat the words.

● Show a card and offer a choice: *rose ou orange ?*

● *Oui ou non ?* (Does the colour you say match the flashcard you show?)

● Ask the children to name the colour you show: *C'est quelle couleur ?* (What colour is it?)

● Finally, combine these new colours with the original six and repeat the questions used before.

● Write up on the board the spelling of the three new colours. Ask which has a silent last letter (*gris*).

● Introduce the final two colours: *brun* (brown) and *violet* (purple). For a change, why not say them and challenge the children to guess their meaning? You could confirm this by showing flashcards 10 and 11.

● Make sure you give the children the chance to practise pronouncing them before you move on.

'Clique, écoute et regarde' (Interactive activity 5)

- This can be used both to consolidate the nine colours the children have already learned and to practise the two new ones: *brun* and *violet*.

- Either select a car to hear the colour pronounced or point to a car and invite the class to provide the colour, confirming (or correcting) their answer by selecting it on the screen.

CD-ROM

- Flashcards 1–11;
- Interactive activity 5: 'Clique, écoute et regarde';
- Interactive activity 6: 'Ecoute et clique'.

'Ecoute et clique' (Interactive activity 6)

- The children hear a colour named and have to click on the car of that colour as it passes.

- This is even more fun if you divide the class into teams and stand a player on each side of the interactive whiteboard.

- The first one to identify the right car gets a point for his or her team.

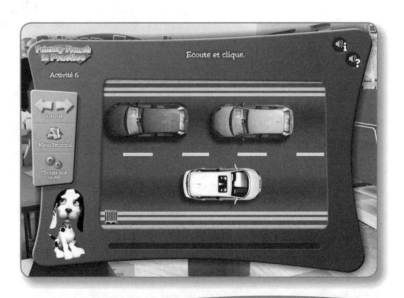

Unit 2 lesson 3

Objective

To consolidate knowledge of colours.

Materials needed

● Colouring pencils or felt-tipped pens;
● 'Jeu des couleurs' photocopiable 8 (page 85).

Starter

● Ask children to name as many colours as they can in French: *Donnez-moi une couleur en français*. You could write them on the board as they are named. In order to ensure that everyone knows the meaning of each colour suggested – and rather than asking for a translation in English – point to something of that colour for the first one named, then encourage a volunteer to do the same for each subsequent colour.

'Qu'est-ce qui manque ?' (Interactive activity 7)

● Play 'Qu'est-ce qui manque ?'. Ask the children to name the six colours on the screen, then press *Enlever* (Remove). They have to answer the question: *Qu'est-ce qui manque ?* (What's missing?) Ask them to guess the meaning of this question rather than telling them.

● When they have identified the missing colour, press *Révéler* (Reveal) to confirm their answer.

● There are ten variations on this game, of which the later examples include numbers as well as colours. After the first few goes, just let them look at the colours without naming them before you remove one.

● Explain the meaning of the word *quelque chose* (something). Then select a child and say *Montre-moi quelque chose de bleu* (Show me something blue). (Note the *de* in the French.) The child must find or point to something blue. Repeat this with different children and different colours.

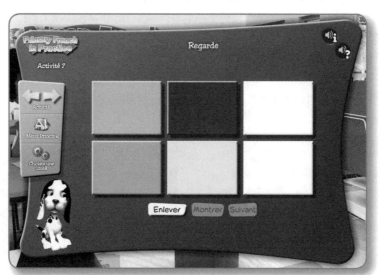

'Jeu des couleurs' (Audio track 4);
'Jeu des couleurs' (Photocopiable page 85)

● Give one sheet to each pair. Tell them they are going to play a game in pairs but first they have to colour in the squares. You could go through the numbers 1–11, telling them orally what colour to fill in for each number:

Un: bleu   *Cinq: vert*   *Neuf: blanc*

Deux: gris   *Six: orange*   *Dix: violet*

Trois: noir   *Sept: jaune*   *Onze: brun*

Quatre: rouge   *Huit: rose*

CD-ROM

● Interactive activity 7: 'Qu'est-ce qui manque ?';
● Audio track 4: 'Jeu des couleurs'.

You could write the list on the board, or do both.

● When they all have their grids ready, introduce the game.

● Explain that you want them to map a journey across the board from the top to the bottom, forming a continuous path of squares. They can move up, down, left or right on the board. Point out the word *Départ* (start) at the top.

● Tell the children you will call a colour from the top row and that is where they must begin. Demonstrate by calling *rouge* and pointing out which box they should be on (display the page on screen from the CD-ROM).

● Next, call *vert* and point to the green box next to it. Then call *rose*, and so on, showing how you are tracing a path over the board.

● Tell them they are now going to hear a set of colours that will take them right to the bottom of the board, where it says *Arrivée* (finish).

● Play the recording, track 4. Pause it when necessary, to give everyone the time to find the right boxes. When they reach the bottom row, encourage them to shout *Arrivée !* Ask who followed the path correctly.

● Repeat the process with the second recording. The path is longer and more complex this time. Again, the children should call *Arrivée !* when they reach the bottom row.

Transcript

Prêts ? (Ready?)

Bleu, orange, jaune, blanc, noir, orange, rose, vert, blanc, bleu, violet, noir, rouge, vert ...

Prêts ?

Orange, vert, rouge, gris, bleu, noir, vert, brun, rose, blanc, violet, gris, bleu, noir, rouge, vert, brun, gris, orange, vert, rouge, blanc, violet, rouge ...

Practice game

● The children can play the 'Jeu des couleurs' game in pairs, one calling the colours and the other tracing the path.

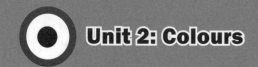

Unit 2 lesson 4

Objectives

- To consolidate knowledge of colours in both oral and written forms.
- To learn how to talk about favourite colours.

Materials needed

- Colouring pencils or felt-tipped pens;
- 'Mots croisés (2)' photocopiable 9 (page 86).

Starter

'Trouve la couleur' (Interactive activity 8)

- Use this quite different game to practise reading the names of the colours.
- The children have to select the right colour to fill in each of the stepping stones across the river.

'Quelle est ta couleur préférée ?' (Audio track 5)

- Now ask the question: *Quelle est ta couleur préférée ?* (What's your favourite colour?) Invite the children to guess what this question means.
- Explain that they are going to hear six French children giving their answer to the question and that they should write down (in English or in French) what each says their favourite colour is.
- Play each question and answer separately. Use the first as an example, replaying it if necessary, to ensure the children understand what they are listening for.
- As you work through the answers one at a time, ask whether they notice anything different about how the French refer to colours (the word *le* is always used with the colour).

Transcript

Teacher:	*Mathieu, quelle est ta couleur préférée ?*
	(Mathieu, what's your favourite colour?)
Mathieu:	*Le vert.*
	(Green.)
Teacher:	*Céline, quelle est ta couleur préférée ?*
	(Céline, what's your favourite colour?)
Céline:	*Le rouge.*
Teacher:	*Youssef, quelle est ta couleur préférée ?*
Youssef:	*L'orange.*
Teacher:	*Marie-Laure, quelle est ta couleur préférée ?*
Marie-Laure:	*Le violet.*
Teacher:	*Benoît, quelle est ta couleur préférée ?*
Benoît:	*Le bleu.*
Teacher:	*Amélie, quelle est ta couleur préférée ?*
Amélie:	*Le rose ou le jaune.*

'Mots croisés (2)' (Photocopiable page 86)

- This sheet provides two activities focusing on the spelling of the colours. The first requires the children to fill in the missing letter in seven colours. This reveals the vertical mystery word – *couleur*.
- The second is a crossword in which they have to provide the full words for seven colours, based on picture clues.

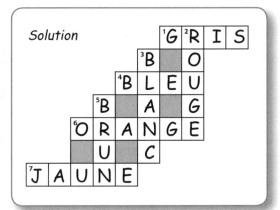

Solution

CD-ROM

- Interactive activity 8: 'Trouve la couleur';
- Audio track 5: 'Quelle est ta couleur préférée ?'.

Practice game

- The children could conduct a survey round the class, asking each other what their favourite colour is. Begin by practising the question, so everyone is confident with the pronunciation, and by reminding them of the *le* that will precede every answer: *le vert, le rouge* and so on.
- If they record the results systematically, you could produce a bar chart showing the class's favourite colours, entitled *Les couleurs préférées de la classe*.

Methodology: putting new vocabulary to use

- It is natural, when introducing the vocabulary of a new topic, to focus at first on individual words. But it is equally important, as soon as the children are confident with that vocabulary, to set it in a meaningful context. There is no point, after all, in their simply being able to point at colours and name them. If possible, include a context which allows them to express something personal about themselves, such as 'favourite colours' above.

- The fish game in the following lesson incorporates the colour adjectives into full sentences. This shows the children for the first time how colour adjectives follow the noun in French. How much you choose to make of this will depend, amongst other things, on how easily you think they will grasp it. In any case, it is best to just let them 'see it happening' at first, before you make a conscious point of it.

Unit 2 lesson 5

Objectives

- To be able to use colour adjectives in full sentences.
- To learn that colour adjectives follow the noun in French.

Materials needed

'Colorie l'image' photocopiable 10 (page 87).

Starter

- You will need to introduce the words *poisson* (fish), *petit* (little) and *gros* (big) if the children have not met them before.

- Do so by drawing a little fish and saying *C'est un poisson.* (This is a fish.) Then elaborate by adding the word *petit*, illustrating its meaning with gestures. Do the same for *gros*.

'Trouve un poisson' (Interactive activity 9)

- Play the game on the whiteboard. The children have to identify fish that fit the descriptions.

- Children or teams could be pitted against each other, to be the first to touch the right fish and score a point.

Transcript

The sentences they hear, in random order, are:

Trouve un gros poisson bleu. (Find a large blue fish.)

Trouve un petit poisson jaune.

Trouve un petit poisson vert.

Trouve un gros poisson blanc.

Trouve un petit poisson rose.

Trouve un gros poisson noir.

Trouve un gros poisson vert.

Trouve un petit poisson bleu.

Trouve un gros poisson jaune.

Trouve un petit poisson orange.

'Colorie l'image' (Photocopiable page 87)

- This is a nice task for children to complete at home. Following the key where each number represents a colour, the children have to colour in the picture.

Practice game

- The children could follow up the task on photocopiable page 87 by preparing a colouring task of their own, creating a line drawing, numbering the spaces and creating a key along the lines of the one on the photocopiable. They could then exchange them for other children to fill in.

CD-ROM

Interactive activity 9: 'Trouve un poisson'.

Recycling the colours vocabulary

Colours can readily be combined with future topics such as the weather (*gris, bleu ...*), clothes, food (*De quelle couleur est une tomate ? ... une banane ?*), pets and personal appearance (eye and hair colour).

To keep the colour words in circulation, why not use them as team names when playing team games: *les rouges, les verts ?*

Unit 3 lesson 1

Objectives

● To learn the words for eight parts of the body, orally.
● To begin to recognise eight parts of the body in written form.

Materials needed

'Le corps' photocopiable 11 (page 88).

Starter

● Begin by pointing to four parts of your body as you name them one at a time: *la tête* (head), *les oreilles* (ears), *les yeux* (eyes), *le nez* (nose). (There is little point in using flashcards when the real thing is readily available to everybody!)

● Children should repeat them after you, pointing at the appropriate parts of themselves. At this stage, don't worry whether they are getting the definite articles (*le, la, les*) right.

● Change the order as you carry on, then say the words, but pause before pointing so children have the chance to show if they know their meaning.

● Next, point to something and let children supply its name.

● Introduce the next four words using the same sequence of activities: *la bouche* (mouth), *les mains* (hands), *le ventre* (tummy), *les pieds* (feet).

● Now tell them you are going to point and say a name. If the name fits what you are pointing at, children should imitate the gesture. If it doesn't, they shouldn't move. Use all eight of the words introduced so far: *la tête, les oreilles, les yeux, le nez, la bouche, les mains, le ventre, les pieds.*

'Rime : la tête, les oreilles … ' (Audio track 6)

● The rhyme should be spoken rhythmically, touching the appropriate parts of the body (which go from top to toe). If you want to sing it, it fits the tune of 'Heads, Shoulders, Knees and Toes' very neatly!

● Allow children to hear the recording several times, if necessary, before they join in. When they get used to it, turn off the recording and let them do it unsupported.

● Children could be asked to learn the rhyme by heart.

Transcript
La tête, les oreilles, les yeux, le nez.
La bouche, les mains, le ventre, les pieds.

'Clique, écoute et répète' (Interactive activity 10)

● This activity showing the *Petit Pont* character Youssef allows you to revise the eight nouns introduced so far (pronounced by a native speaker) and to practise them in a new way.

● Name a part of Youssef for a volunteer to identify. When they touch it, the written word will appear to confirm their choice and to reinforce the spelling.

CD-ROM

● Audio track 6: 'Rime : la tête, les oreilles … ';
● Interactive activity 10: 'Clique, écoute et répète'.

'Le corps' (Photocopiable page 88)

● Give each child a sheet with the picture of Mathieu and ask them to draw in lines *in pencil* to link the labels to the correct parts of his body. You may feel you want to present the written form in conjunction with the spoken form before asking them to read it. But why not challenge them to see if they can work this out for themselves?

● The words are positioned to left and right so they can subsequently cover them over and test themselves at saying the name of the thing that each line leads to.

● This may be the first time they have seen the circumflex accent in *tête*. Point out that this, like the acute accent they met earlier, is a part of the spelling.

Methodology: *le*, *la* and *les*

● At some point you will need to confront the phenomenon of gender in French and the fact that every noun is either masculine or feminine.

● If you are following this sequence of lesson plans with absolute beginners, this is probably not the best point at which to draw attention to the grammar involved.

● If children notice it and ask about it, on the other hand, it would be wrong not to satisfy their curiosity with at least a brief explanation.

● The fact that the word for 'the' changes according to whether you are talking about one or more things is also different from English, though common to other European languages.

Unit 3 lesson 2

Objectives

● To be able to sing a French rap with actions.
● To begin to recognise the instructions *touche, ouvre* and *ferme*.

Materials needed

'Rap' photocopiable 12 (page 89).

Starter

● Tell the children to say the name in French as you touch your head, eyes, nose, ears, mouth, hands, tummy and feet one after the other – slowly at first then faster and faster until the children can only just keep up.

● Begin by mouthing the word if they need help.

'Rap : un, deux … ' (Audio track 7); 'Rap' (Photocopiable page 89)

● The words of this rap are based on the vocabulary previously learned, plus the imperatives *touche* (touch), *ferme* (close) and *ouvre* (open). It should be accompanied by actions.

● Introduce these new words by demonstrating with a door or pencil case. Once you've illustrated the meanings a few times ask the children to supply the correct word to the action until they are secure with the new vocabulary.

● The rap involves children closing and opening their eyes while singing and requires a considerable amount of concentration, thereby generating a lot of fun. A gesture with each hand can accompany the words '*Un, deux*'.

● Play the first verse of the rap.

● Play it a second time, demonstrating the actions that go with it.

● Play the first verse again, asking children to do the actions themselves.

● You could introduce the children to the written form of the song using the lyrics on photocopiable page 89.

Transcript

Un, deux.
Un, deux.
Touche ta bouche.
Ferme les yeux.

Un, deux.
Un, deux.
Touche ta tête.
Ouvre les yeux.

Un, deux.
Un, deux.
Touche ton nez.
Ferme les yeux.

Un, deux.
Un, deux.
Touche tes oreilles.
Ouvre les yeux.

Un, deux.
Un, deux.
Touche tes pieds.
Ferme les yeux.

Un, deux.
Un, deux.
Touche ton ventre.
Ouvre les yeux.

'Rap : un, deux … ' (Interactive activity 11)

- The song can also be learned using the karaoke-style presentation on the CD-ROM, in which the words are highlighted as they are sung. It can be paused after each phrase, or at any point you like.

CD-ROM

- Audio track 7: 'Rap: un, deux … ';
- Interactive activity 11: 'Rap: un, deux … '.

A point of grammar

The instructions referring to actions that you can only do to yourself (opening or closing your eyes) use the word les, precisely because it's considered obvious whose eyes you are talking about. With the other instructions about touching parts of the body ('touch your head', 'touch your feet', and so on) the possessive pronoun ton, ta or tes is used, because you could be touching somebody else's. (Note, it is not suggested that you enter into this subtlety with children.)

Practice game

- You can now play 'Jacques a dit' ('Simon says') using the same instructions:

Touche ta bouche.	Touche ton nez.
Ouvre les yeux.	Touche tes oreilles.
Ferme les yeux.	Touche tes pieds.
Touche ta tête.	Touche ton ventre.

- Children carry out the commands only if these are preceded by the words Jacques a dit. Although this is traditionally a competitive game, they do not necessarily have to drop out if they get it wrong.

Unit 3 lesson 3

Objective

To be able to use colour words with vocabulary for parts of the body.

Materials needed

● Colouring pencils or felt-tipped pens;
● 'Un robot et un monstre' photocopiable 13 (page 90).

Starter

● Tell the class that they are going to draw a face. Draw an oval on the board, then ask a child to come up, give them the pen and ask them to draw the eyes: *Dessine les yeux.*

● Ask another to draw the mouth, the ears and the nose. Each time ask the rest of the class: *C'est bon ?* The result will probably be quite funny!

● You could do this several times. The third or fourth time, a child could give the instructions.

'Ecoute et colorie le clown' (Interactive activity 12)

● The children have to colour in the different parts of the clown with the right colours. The last instruction is: *Colorie son chapeau en noir.* (Colour the hat black.)

● Invite children to guess the meaning of the word *chapeau,* allowing them to discover who was right by selecting the right colour and watching the animation.

● Now introduce the words for arms and legs: *les bras* and *les jambes.* Practise these briefly, writing them on the board once children are used to the pronunciation.

● Point out that the final 's' on both is silent. You could also point out that the word *bras* means both 'arm' and 'arms', getting no extra 's' as it already ends in one.

'Un robot et un monstre' (Photocopiable page 90)

- Begin by reading the name of the activity and asking children what they notice about the words *robot* and *monstre* themselves. (They look similar to English but there are differences in spelling and pronunciation – such as the silent 't' at the end of *robot*.)

- Ask the children to colour the two drawings according to the instructions. These recycle all the 'parts of the body' vocabulary introduced so far, including *bras* and *jambes*. You will need to explain the final instruction: *Colorie le reste comme tu veux*. (Colour in the rest as you want.)

- Now ask them to look at the six statements about the drawings, which combine numbers with parts of the body. Read through at least the first two together, asking the children to suggest what they mean. You will need to explain that *a* means 'has'.

- Explain that they must decide whether each of the sentences is true, answering '*oui*' ou '*non*'. Depending on the class, you may then want to let them try the others on their own. If you do, go through them all together once everyone has finished.

> **CD-ROM**
>
> Interactive activity 12: 'Ecoute et colorie le clown'.

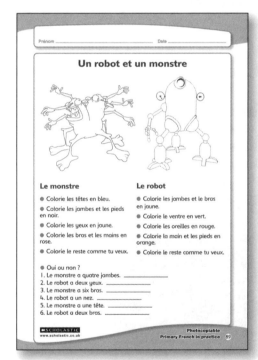

Answers
1: *oui*
2: *non*
3: *oui*
4: *non*
5: *non*
6: *non*

Practice game

- Invite the children to invent a similar sentence of their own about one of the drawings. For example: *Le robot a deux oreilles*. They should then work in pairs, taking turns to make up a sentence: their partner has to decide whether or not it is true.

- Demonstrate with one child, repeating the example you have given and eliciting the answer *oui* or *non*.

- While they are doing this, circulate in the classroom, giving support and correcting any major mistakes.

Unit 3 lesson 4

Objective

To be able to describe a fantasy drawing using numbers and parts of the body.

Materials needed

● Colouring pencils or felt-tipped pens;
● 'Qu'est-ce qui manque ?' photocopiable 14 (page 91).

Starter

● Play the game in which children draw a named part of a body then pass the picture on for the next person to add a part, and so on.

● Give each child a sheet of paper and tell them they are going to draw a monster, one part at a time.

● Begin by telling them to *dessinez les yeux* (draw the eyes). Don't give them more than 10 seconds to do this. Then tell everyone to *passez-le* (pass it on). On the sheet they have now received, tell them to *dessinez le nez* (draw the nose). Continue with the following parts of the body: *la bouche* (mouth), *la tête* (head), *les oreilles* (ears), *les bras* (arms), *les mains* (hands), *le ventre* (tummy), *les jambes* (legs), *les pieds* (feet).

● When the drawings have been completed, collect them in and show them one at a time at the front of the class.

'Fais un bonhomme de neige' (Interactive activity 13)

● First, introduce the new expression *un bonhomme de neige* (a snowman), then open the activity on the interactive whiteboard and ask them to guess what it means.

● The children can take turns to select and add a part of the snowman. Encourage them to guess the meaning of *choisis* (choose) and *une écharpe* (a scarf). See if they can remember what *chapeau* (hat) means (they came across the word in the clown activity). When they have finished, they can make another snowman. Like the other interactive games, this is something children could do on their own afterwards.

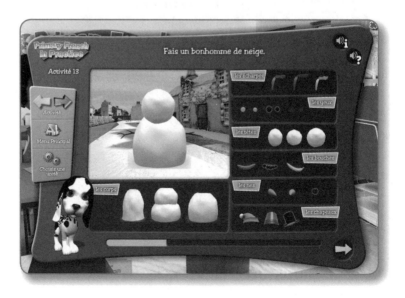

'Qu'est-ce qui manque?' (Photocopiable page 91)

- This page provides writing practice of the parts of the body in a fun context.

- The children have to write the names of the parts missing from the pirate, the statue, the shop window dummy, the scarecrow and the snowman.

> Answers
> 1: *jambe, main*
> 2: *bras, nez*
> 3: *pieds, mains, tête*
> 4: *mains, pieds*
> 5: *bras, nez, oreilles, bouche*

Practice games

- Say the rhyme (Audio track 6: 'Rime : la tête, les oreilles … '). Some children may like to do it at the front of the class, with the challenge of opening and closing their eyes and doing all the actions at the right times.

- The obvious context for the unit of parts of the body is describing people's appearance – particularly eye and hair colour. This, though, involves a more difficult sentence structure (*Il/elle a les yeux bleus* et *les cheveux blonds*, for example) and is best left to a later date. In any case, it is important not to use up all the potential of a unit, as coming back to it in a fresh context is what will keep it alive in children's minds.

CD-ROM

- Interactive activity 13: 'Fais un bonhomme de neige';
- Audio track 6: 'Rime : la tête, les oreilles … ' (optional).

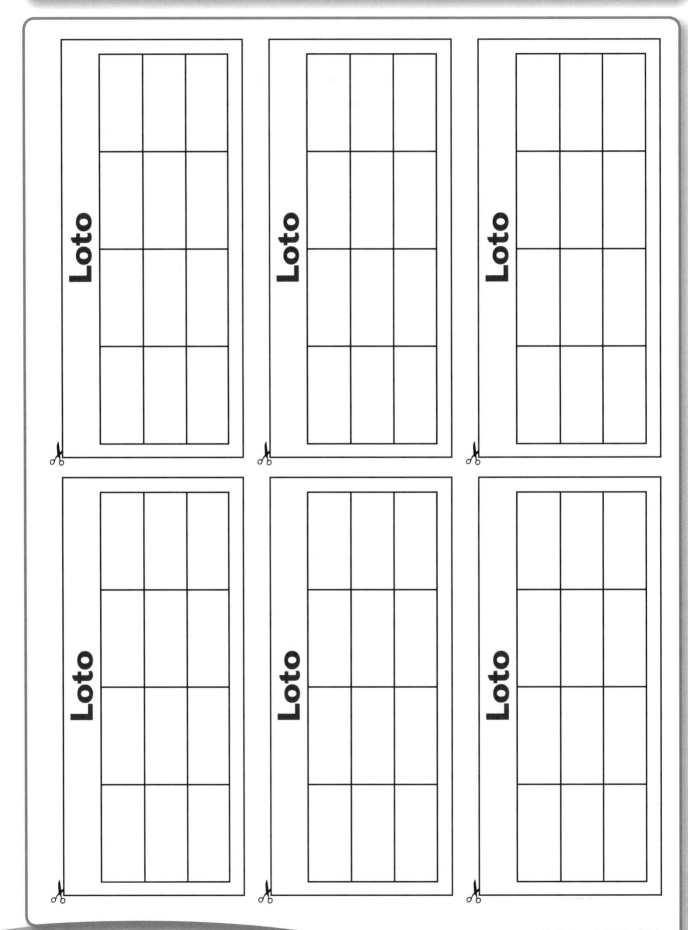

■ SCHOLASTIC
www.scholastic.co.uk

Les nombres

 un	 deux	 trois
 quatre	 cinq	 six
 sept	 huit	 neuf
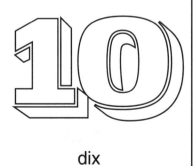 dix		

Dix euros

Dix euros,
Ça ne va pas loin.
Prends un pain au chocolat.
Il te reste combien ?

Neuf euros,
Ça ne va pas loin.
Prends un pain au chocolat.
Il te reste combien ?

Huit euros,
Ça ne va pas loin.
Prends un pain au chocolat.
Il te reste combien ?

Sept euros,
Ça ne va pas loin.
Prends un pain au chocolat.
Il te reste combien ?

Six euros,
Ça ne va pas loin.
Prends un pain au chocolat.
Il te reste combien ?

Cinq euros,
Ça ne va pas loin.
Prends un pain au chocolat.
Il te reste combien ?

Quatre euros,
Ça ne va pas loin.
Prends un pain au chocolat.
Il te reste combien ?

Trois euros,
Ça ne va pas loin.
Prends un pain au chocolat.
Il te reste combien ?

Deux euros,
Ça ne va pas loin.
Prends un pain au chocolat.
Il te reste combien ?

Un euro,
Ça ne va pas loin.
Prends un pain au chocolat.
Il ne te reste rien !

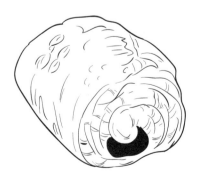 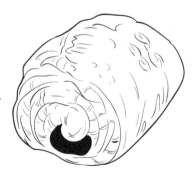 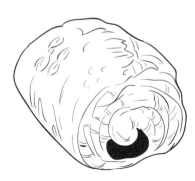

Découvre le numéro !

- Join up the numbers listed to reveal the hidden number.
- Write the name of the number on the dotted line.

1.

•7
•4
•1   •5
•3
•6
•2   •8
•9
•0
•10

dix – sept – quatre

Réponse: _ _ _ _ _ _ _ _ _ _ _ _ _ _

2.

•6   •5
•2
•7
•1 •10 •4
•11
•8
•3
•9

six – cinq – dix – quatre –
un – dix – trois

Réponse: _ _ _ _ _ _ _ _ _ _ _ _ _ _ _

3.

•0
•4   •6
•2
•5
•10
•1
•7
•3
•12
•8
•9   •11

neuf – onze – huit – trois –
un – dix – six - quatre

Réponse: _ _ _ _ _ _ _ _ _ _ _ _ _ _

4.

•10   •1
•4
•11
•2   •0
•9
•3
•8

zéro – deux – onze –
quatre – dix – un – huit

Réponse: _ _ _ _ _ _ _ _ _ _ _ _ _ _

Calculs

1. Neuf – six = _____

2. Sept + quatre = _____

3. Deux + trois + quatre = _____

4. Douze – dix = _____

5. Six + quatre = _____

6. Cinq + six = _____

7. Neuf – trois + six = _____

8. Sept + cinq = _____

9. Dix – trois = _____

10. Un + deux + trois + six – douze = _____

Mots croisés (1)

● Write in the French numbers 1 to 12!

un deux trois quatre cinq six sept huit neuf dix onze douze

Jeu

● Jetez deux dés

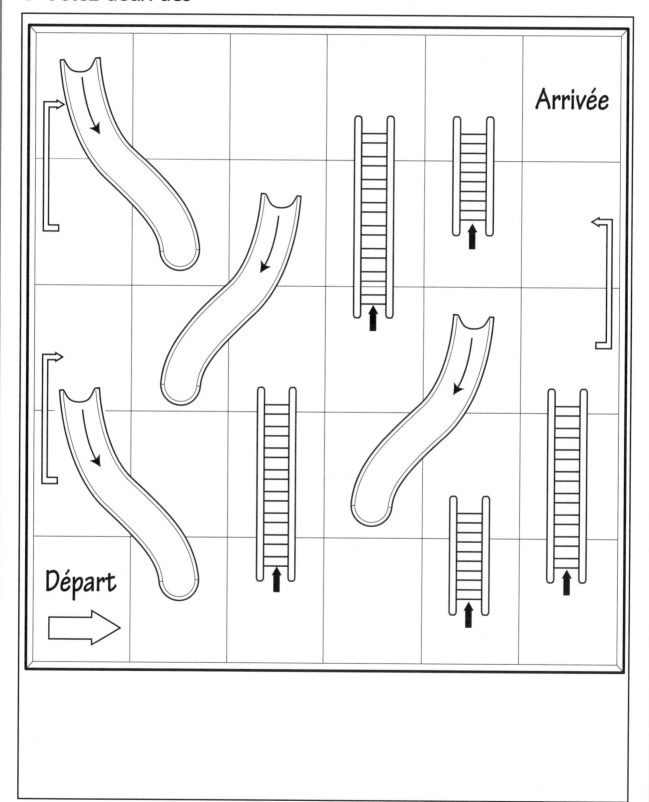

◼ SCHOLASTIC
www.scholastic.co.uk

Jeu des couleurs

- Colorie les cases, puis joue au jeu.
- Directions de jeu : ← → ↑ ↓

//////////////////////// **Départ** ////////////////////////

1	2	3	4	5	6	7
6	7	1	2	8	9	10
4	9	3	5	11	7	2
5	8	6	7	9	3	1
9	1	10	11	5	4	11
8	4	3	2	6	9	10
10	5	7	1	3	8	4

 ▮▮▮▮▮ ▮▮▮▮▮ *Arrivée!* ▮▮▮▮▮ ▮▮▮▮▮

Mots croisés (2)

● Fill in the missing letters to find the mystery word. What do you think it means? _____

B	L	A	N					
					R	A	N	G	E
	J	A		N	E	
		B		E	U	
		V		R	T	
	R	O		G	E	
N	O	I	

● Write in the colours.

I.

4, 3, 2.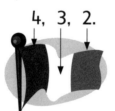

5.

6.

7.

Colorie l'image

1 bleu
2 rouge
3 jaune
4 vert
5 rose
6 noir
7 orange
8 violet
9 brun
10 gris

Le corps

- Relie les mots aux parties du corps. (Join up the words to the parts of the body.)

la tête

exemple

les yeux

les oreilles

la bouche

le nez

les mains

le ventre

les pieds

Rap

Un, deux...

Un, deux.
Un, deux.
Touche ta bouche.
Ferme les yeux.

Un, deux.
Un, deux.
Touche ta tête.
Ouvre les yeux.

Un, deux.
Un, deux.
Touche ton nez.
Ferme les yeux.

Un, deux.
Un, deux.
Touche tes oreilles.
Ouvre les yeux.

Un, deux.
Un, deux.
Touche tes pieds.
Ferme les yeux.

Un, deux.
Un, deux.
Touche ton ventre.
Ouvre les yeux.

Un robot et un monstre

 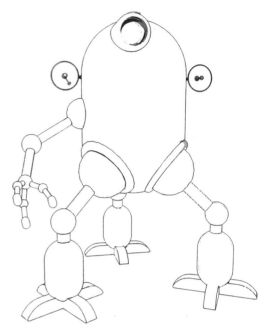

Le monstre

● Colorie les têtes en bleu.

● Colorie les jambes et les pieds en noir.

● Colorie les yeux en jaune.

● Colorie les bras et les mains en rose.

● Colorie le reste comme tu veux.

Le robot

● Colorie les jambes et le bras en jaune.

● Colorie le ventre en vert.

● Colorie les oreilles en rouge.

● Colorie la main et les pieds en orange.

● Colorie le reste comme tu veux.

● Oui ou non ?

1. Le monstre a quatre jambes. _____

2. Le robot a deux yeux. _____

3. Le monstre a six bras. _____

4. Le robot a un nez. _____

5. Le monstre a une tête. _____

6. Le robot a deux bras. _____

Qu'est-ce qui manque ?

● Write in the names for the parts of their bodies that are missing!

1.

jambe
_____

2.

_____

3.

4.

5.

_____   _____   _____

Key factors for success

If you are just starting to teach French to primary children, it is as well to be aware of some of the challenges and responsibilities that lie ahead. You have the good fortune to be teaching an age group that is naturally receptive to languages. Not only is the subject new to them but many of the activities you introduce them to will be new as well. This makes the task for their teachers at secondary school all the more challenging, since they won't have this advantage of novelty. For the sake of both your pupils and their future teachers, therefore, it is important to equip children with as solid a foundation as possible.

How to build a solid foundation

- Avoid making French seem a 'lightweight' subject, full of fun games but little substance.

- Don't avoid the grammar out of concern that it is 'more demanding' or will put children off. If they can get used to thinking about how the language works from the outset, the stigma so often attached to grammar at a later stage may be avoided.

- Ensure that they are following a coherent scheme of work, so they can feel their competence and knowledge growing. There should be no major gaps of understanding for them to fall down.

- Concentrate on building their confidence, especially with spoken French. This will enable them to tackle more interesting things at the next stage and avoid the 'kiss of death' effect of having to go back again over all the basic topics and language.

- Ensure you systematically recycle vocabulary they have learned before so they don't just forget it. Lesson starters provide a good opportunity for this.

- Explore the possibilities of integrating French with other areas of the curriculum (CLIL: Content and Language Integrated Learning).

- Consider using a formal assessment scheme such as *The Languages Ladder* (see page 40) to give children a sense of their own progress.

- Take an active interest in the transition from primary to secondary. The smoother this can be, the better the chance of maintaining children's motivation and the more likely they will be to continue with what you have started.

How to keep your teaching fresh and stimulating

- Keep a 'hit list' or menu of activity types that you use and find effective. It is easy to forget a good game or routine. It is equally easy to overuse certain activities just out of habit.

- Working on and improving your own French will in itself keep you fresh, enabling you to say and do new things in your lessons. Being a learner at the same time as being a teacher can be a very positive experience.

- Take every opportunity to share ideas and experiences with colleagues. A useful tip or resource can be very welcome – particularly for a subject in which you are not a specialist.

- Look for opportunities to use French outside the French lesson itself. The more often you and the children hear, speak or read it, the more natural it will become.

- Make the most of significant events in the French calendar:

- If at all possible, set up a link with a French (or French-speaking) primary school. Such links not only make the whole experience of using the language more real and purposeful, they also provide a fertile source of authentic material. Topics previously covered – such as age, family and pets – suddenly take on a new lease of life!

Events in the French calendar

Nouvel an (New Year's Day)

La fête des rois (6 January – the Festival of Kings)

Saint Valentin (14 February – Valentine's Day)

Pâques (Easter)

La fête des mères (Mothers' day) in early May

La fête nationale/Le 14 juillet (14 July – Bastille Day)

Les grandes vacances (the summer holiday)

La rentrée (the beginning of the school year – a major event in France)

Halloween (only recently adopted in France but already very popular with children)

Noël (Christmas)

Recommended further reading

Plenty of published resources and others available on the internet include materials relating to cultural and current events in France. *La Petite Presse*, being a quarterly publication specifically for primary French, lends itself particularly well to such cultural topics and regularly features festivals and customs from other francophone countries as well as France.

The following websites and publications can provide useful information and support:

The *Key Stage 2 Framework for Languages* can be downloaded from: www.standards.dfes.gov.uk/primary/publications/languages/framework

The QCA *Scheme of Work for French* can be downloaded from: www.qca.org.uk/qca_11752.aspx

Information about primary languages, including courses to improve your own French, is available at: www.nacell.org.uk

The training zone for KS2 languages is an excellent source of ideas and includes lots of video clips from real lessons: www.primarylanguages. org.uk

The *Young Pathfinders* series, published by CILT, provides good, practical advice and support on specific areas of language teaching:

- *Games and Fun Activities*, by Cynthia Martin
- *Are You Sitting Comfortably? Telling Stories to Young Language Learners*, by Daniel Tierney and Patricia Dobson
- *Speak Up! Using the Target Language in Class*, by Peter Satchwell and June de Silva
- *First Steps to Reading and Writing*, by Christina Skarbek
- *Let's Join In! Rhymes, Poems and Songs*, by Cynthia Martin and Catherine Cheater
- *Making the Link: Teaching Languages to Young Learners in Different Subjects,* by Daniel Tierney and Malcolm Hope

- *Grammar is Fun*, by Lydia Biriotti
- *The Literacy Link*, by Catherine Cheater and Anne Farren
- *A World of Languages! Developing Children's Love of Languages*, by Manjula Datta and Cathy Pomphrey
- *A Flying Start! Introducing Early Language Learning*, by Peter Satchwell and June de Silva
- *Mind the Gap! Improving Transition between Key Stage 2 and 3*, by Rosemary Bevis and Ann Gregory
- *We Have the Technology: Using ICT to Enhance Primary Languages*, by Therese Comfort and Daniel Tierney
- *Working Together: Native Speakers in the Primary School*, by Cynthia Martin and Anne Farren

The following DVD, published by CILT, shows many examples of good practice: *Early Language Learning: Making it Happen, Making it Work and Making it Better*.

For information about assessment using *The Languages Ladder*, go to:
www.teachernet.gov.uk/languagesladder
www.assetlanguages.org.uk